The New Power 2024: Politics in Mexico

King Rojo

DEDICATION

This book, "The New Power 2024: Politics in Mexico," is dedicated with profound gratitude and heartfelt appreciation to the people of Mexico. It is a tribute to the resilience, courage, and unwavering spirit of the Mexican citizens who have contributed to the nation's journey towards a better future.

This book is dedicated to the voices that often go unheard—the marginalized communities, the indigenous peoples, and the vulnerable populations of Mexico. Your resilience and perseverance in the face of adversity inspire us all to continue striving for a society that leaves no one behind.

With deep appreciation and utmost respect,

King Rojo.

CONTENTS

The New Power in Action

ACKNOWLEDGMENTS

Writing a book is a collaborative effort, and "The New Power 2024: Politics in Mexico" would not have been possible without the support, encouragement, and contributions of numerous individuals and organizations. In this chapter, we express our heartfelt gratitude to all those who have played a significant role in making this book a reality.

INTRODUCTION

THE NEW POWER 2024 - POLITICS IN MEXICO

In the year 2024, Mexico stands at a critical juncture in its political history, a defining moment that holds the potential to reshape the nation's trajectory for years to come. As the world navigates an ever-changing landscape of challenges and opportunities, Mexico finds itself grappling with its own unique set of complexities, seeking to forge a new path forward amid a rapidly transforming global order.

"The New Power 2024: Politics in Mexico" explores the dynamic interplay of political forces, institutions, and societal aspirations that have shaped the country's past and continue to influence its future. With a steadfast focus on Mexico's political landscape, this book delves into the complexities of governance, the pursuit of democracy, and the pressing issues confronting Mexican society.

Understanding Mexico's political evolution requires tracing its historical roots. From ancient civilizations to Spanish conquests and post-independence struggles, the country's journey has been marked by resilience and tenacity. Our exploration begins with an insightful historical overview, providing a solid foundation for comprehending the forces that shaped modern-day Mexico.

At the heart of Mexico's political machinery lies its presidency. We delve into the pivotal role of the president and the executive powers wielded, examining the current administration's policies, promises, and challenges. Concurrently, we unravel the inner workings of the Mexican Congress, a critical legislative entity instrumental in shaping the nation's laws and policies.

The rule of law and an independent judiciary form the bedrock of any thriving democracy. Throughout the book, we investigate the state of the Mexican judiciary, its autonomy, and landmark legal cases that have indelibly influenced politics and society.

Mexico's journey towards progress is not devoid of hurdles. Corruption casts a long shadow over the political landscape, demanding earnest efforts to root it out. We analyze the impact of corruption on governance and explore the effectiveness of anti-corruption initiatives in fostering transparency and accountability.

Safety and security constitute another central challenge, with Mexico confronting issues of crime and violence. We examine the nation's ongoing battle against drug cartels and explore strategies to enhance public safety while protecting human rights.

Economic policies and social welfare are integral components of the Mexican political discourse. Assessing economic challenges and opportunities, we scrutinize the government's efforts to alleviate poverty and promote social welfare programs to uplift the marginalized sections of society.

As we venture into the realm of education and youth empowerment, we explore the transformational potential of educational reforms and delve into empowering the youth to become active participants in shaping Mexico's future.

Elections serve as the bedrock of democratic representation. Our exploration of political parties and electoral dynamics sheds light on the factors that influence voter behavior and turnout, shaping the outcomes that determine the course of Mexico's political journey.

Beyond national borders, we investigate Mexico's role on the global stage. Unraveling its foreign policy and diplomatic engagements, we assess the nation's standing in the international community and the challenges and opportunities it encounters in an interconnected world.

Throughout the book, we showcase the power of grassroots movements and civil society initiatives in effecting positive change. Additionally, we examine the media landscape and its impact on political discourse, emphasizing the need for responsible journalism and information integrity.

As we culminate this comprehensive exploration, we envision a Mexico propelled by the force of the new power - an enlightened, dynamic, and transformative force that draws from the collective will of its citizens. "The New Power 2024: Politics in Mexico" endeavors to foster understanding, provoke thought, and inspire action, empowering readers to become active participants in shaping the future of this remarkable nation.

Join us on this transformative journey as we embark on an exploration of Mexico's political landscape and the promise of a new era, "The New Power 2024."

UNDERSTANDING MEXICO'S POLITICAL EVOLUTION

Mexico's political evolution is a tapestry woven with threads of resilience, revolution, and reform. From its ancient civilizations to the present day, the nation's history has been shaped by conquests, colonization, and struggles for independence, leaving an indelible mark on its political landscape. Understanding the complexities of Mexico's political evolution is crucial for comprehending the forces that have shaped its present and the potential pathways it may follow in the future.

Ancient Civilizations: The Seeds of Political Thought

Long before the arrival of Spanish conquistadors, the land we now know as Mexico was home to advanced civilizations. The Aztecs, Mayans, and other indigenous groups thrived, building sophisticated societies with rich cultural, political, and religious traditions. The remnants of these ancient civilizations still resonate in modern Mexican identity, providing a foundation for the values and aspirations that shape the nation's political landscape today.

Spanish Conquest and Colonial Rule

In 1519, Hernán Cortés and his expeditionary forces embarked on a journey that would forever alter Mexico's destiny. The Spanish conquest led to the fall of the Aztec empire and the imposition of colonial rule. For nearly three centuries, Mexico was part of the vast Spanish empire, subjected to a hierarchical political system and exploitation of its resources. This era laid the groundwork for a stark social divide and shaped the struggle for independence that lay ahead.

The Struggle for Independence

The spark of independence was ignited on September 16, 1810, with Miguel Hidalgo's famous "Grito de Dolores." The cry for freedom set in motion a prolonged struggle against Spanish rule. The heroes of the Mexican War of Independence, such as Hidalgo, Morelos, and Allende, fought valiantly to secure liberty and self-determination for the Mexican people. On September 27, 1821, Mexico achieved its independence, marking the beginning of a new chapter in its political history.

The Early Republic and Political Turmoil

Following independence, Mexico faced considerable challenges in forging a stable political system. The nation experienced a series of political transitions, including the First Mexican Empire, which gave way to the First Mexican Republic. Turmoil and instability marred the early years of the republic, as regional factions vied for power, leading to a pattern of political upheaval that would persist for decades.

The Porfiriato: Authoritarianism and Modernization

In the latter half of the 19th century, General Porfirio Díaz emerged as a dominant figure in Mexican politics. The Porfiriato, as his rule became known, was characterized by economic modernization and industrialization, but also by political repression and authoritarianism. Although Díaz sought stability and progress, his long rule sowed the seeds of discontent that would ultimately lead to the Mexican Revolution.

The Mexican Revolution: A Turning Point

The Mexican Revolution, which began in 1910, marked a profound turning point in Mexico's political history. Led by figures such as Francisco Madero, Emiliano Zapata, and Pancho Villa, the revolution sought to overthrow the Díaz regime and address social and economic injustices. The revolution's outcomes were multifaceted, leading to constitutional reforms, land redistribution, and a new sense of national identity grounded in the principles of justice and equality.

The Institutional Revolutionary Party (PRI) Era

Following the Mexican Revolution, the Institutional Revolutionary Party (PRI) emerged as the dominant political force in Mexico. The PRI governed the nation for over seven decades, maintaining stability through a mixture of authoritarianism, co-optation, and pragmatic policies. Under the PRI's rule, Mexico experienced periods of economic growth, but also faced challenges of corruption, political repression, and uneven distribution of wealth.

Towards Democracy: The Transition and Beyond

In the late 20th century, Mexico embarked on a path towards democratization. The 1988 presidential election marked a significant moment when the PRI's historical dominance was challenged, leading to the rise of opposition parties. Subsequent years witnessed greater political pluralism, free and fair elections, and a gradual transition towards a more democratic system.

Mexico's political evolution is a mosaic of triumphs and struggles, characterized by perseverance and a quest for justice. Understanding the nation's past provides a lens through which we can analyze its present political dynamics and envisage the possibilities for the future. As Mexico enters the year 2024, the seeds sown by its ancient civilizations, the struggles for independence, the revolutions, and the transitions towards democracy converge to shape "The New Power" that beckons the nation forward. In the chapters that follow, we will delve deeper into Mexico's contemporary political landscape, exploring its institutions, challenges, and the potential for transformation in the pursuit of a better tomorrow.

HISTORICAL OVERVIEW OF MEXICAN POLITICS

To understand the present, one must delve into the past. The historical roots of Mexican politics are deeply intertwined with its rich tapestry of civilizations, conquests, revolutions, and reforms. This chapter embarks on a journey through the annals of time, exploring the key events, milestones, and political movements that have shaped Mexico's political landscape. From the pre-Columbian era to the dawn of the 21st century, the echoes of history reverberate in the institutions and aspirations of modern-day Mexico.

The Pre-Columbian Civilizations

Long before European contact, the land now known as Mexico was home to advanced civilizations that flourished across its diverse regions. The Olmecs, Maya, and Aztecs were among the most influential, building thriving societies with complex political structures, sophisticated urban centers, and rich cultural traditions. The remnants of their legacies continue to resonate in modern Mexican identity, laying the groundwork for the principles of governance and community that endure to this day.

The Spanish Conquest and Colonial Rule

The year 1519 marked a momentous turning point in Mexican history when the Spanish conquistadors, led by Hernán Cortés, arrived on its shores. Over the following years, the Aztec Empire, then a dominant force in the region, succumbed to Spanish conquest, leading to the establishment of New Spain. Colonial rule imposed a hierarchical political system, with the Spanish crown exercising absolute authority over its subjects. This period witnessed the fusion of Spanish and indigenous cultures, creating a unique mestizo identity that characterizes Mexican society.

Independence and the Birth of a Nation

The early 19th century saw Mexico embark on a journey towards independence. Inspired by the ideals of liberty and self-determination, revolutionaries such as Miguel Hidalgo, José María Morelos, and Vicente Guerrero led the charge against Spanish colonial rule. On September 27, 1821, Mexico achieved its independence, marking the birth of a sovereign nation. The newly independent Mexico struggled to establish stable governance structures, leading to a series of political transitions and upheavals.

The Liberal Reform and the Era of Reform

In the mid-19th century, Mexico underwent significant political and social transformations during the Liberal Reform. Led by figures such as Benito Juárez, this era sought to secularize society, break the power of the Catholic Church, and promote individual liberties. The Reform Laws of the 1850s laid the groundwork for the separation of church and state, land redistribution, and the introduction of liberal principles into the country's legal framework.

Porfirian Era: Stability and Authoritarianism

The late 19th and early 20th centuries witnessed the Porfiriato, a period of stability and economic growth under the rule of Porfirio Díaz. Although Díaz's regime brought modernization and development to Mexico, it was marked by political repression and growing social inequalities. The concentration of power in the hands of a few elites eventually led to widespread discontent and set the stage for the Mexican Revolution.

The Mexican Revolution: A Struggle for Justice

The Mexican Revolution, which erupted in 1910, remains one of the most pivotal periods in Mexican history. Fueled by a desire for land reform, workers' rights, and social justice, the revolution saw a diverse array of leaders, including Francisco Madero, Emiliano Zapata, and Pancho Villa, unite to challenge the Porfirian regime. This revolution culminated in the drafting of the Constitution of 1917, which laid the foundation for modern Mexican governance and incorporated progressive social and labor reforms.

The Dominance of the Institutional Revolutionary Party (PRI)

In the post-revolutionary period, the Institutional Revolutionary Party (PRI) emerged as the dominant political force in Mexico. The PRI governed the nation for over seven decades, employing a combination of co-optation, populism, and authoritarianism to maintain its hold on power. The party's hegemony, however, eventually sparked demands for greater political pluralism and democratic reforms.

The Path to Democracy: Mexico in the 20th Century

Throughout the 20th century, Mexico witnessed gradual strides towards democratization. In the latter half of the century, opposition movements, social unrest, and international pressures contributed to the opening of political space. The 1988 presidential election, in particular, marked a significant shift towards electoral competitiveness and paved the way for multi-party politics in Mexico.

The historical overview of Mexican politics serves as a backdrop against which the current political landscape can be understood. The legacy of ancient civilizations, the struggle for independence, the triumphs and challenges of nation-building, and the quest for social justice have all contributed to shaping Mexico's political identity. As the nation approaches the year 2024, this historical understanding sets the stage for a deeper exploration of the challenges and opportunities that lie ahead in "The New Power" era of Mexican politics.

TRANSITION TO DEMOCRACY AND CURRENT POLITICAL LANDSCAPE

The dawn of the 21st century ushered in a new era of political transformation in Mexico. After decades of single-party dominance and authoritarian rule under the Institutional Revolutionary Party (PRI), the country embarked on a path towards democratization. The process of transitioning to democracy was marked by challenges, social movements, and the emergence of new political actors. This chapter delves into the pivotal moments of Mexico's democratization journey and explores the current political landscape that shapes the nation as it approaches the year 2024.

The Winds of Change: Mexico's Democratic Transition

The 1988 presidential election proved to be a turning point in Mexican politics. Amidst allegations of electoral fraud, a vibrant opposition movement emerged, coalescing around Cuauhtémoc Cárdenas of the National Democratic Front. Although the PRI claimed victory, the election ignited calls for electoral reform and greater political openness.

In the following years, Mexico witnessed a gradual process of political liberalization. Pressure from civil society, international actors, and internal factions within the PRI contributed to opening up the political system. Key constitutional reforms in 1996 and 1997 paved the way for competitive elections and the creation of the Federal Electoral Institute (IFE), later transformed into the National Electoral Institute (INE), to ensure electoral integrity and oversee the democratic process.

The End of Single-Party Rule: The 2000 Presidential Election

The year 2000 marked a historic moment in Mexican politics with the presidential election that resulted in the PRI's defeat. Vicente Fox of the National Action Party (PAN) emerged as the victor, ending over seven decades of single-party rule. The peaceful transfer of power to an opposition party signaled the consolidation of Mexico's democratic transition.

Challenges and Opportunities of the Democratic Era

Despite the triumph of the democratic transition, challenges persisted. The PAN's subsequent administrations, followed by a return to PRI rule under Enrique Peña Nieto, faced issues such as corruption, crime, and economic disparities. Moreover, deeply ingrained power structures and practices from the past continued to influence Mexican politics.

In this democratic era, new political actors emerged. The left-leaning National Regeneration Movement (MORENA), led by Andrés Manuel López Obrador (AMLO), gained momentum as a force for change. AMLO's populist message resonated with many Mexicans, leading to his election as president in 2018. His presidency represented a seismic shift in Mexican politics and raised expectations for transformative governance.

The AMLO Presidency: Promises and Challenges

As the first left-wing president in recent Mexican history, AMLO pledged to address corruption, tackle crime, reduce social inequalities, and promote inclusive economic growth. His administration sought to prioritize the needs of the poor and marginalized, promising a "Fourth Transformation" of the nation. However, critics voiced concerns about the concentration of power, the erosion of checks and balances, and the government's approach to certain policies, including energy and security.

The Political Landscape in 2024

As Mexico approaches the year 2024, the political landscape continues to evolve. The 2021 midterm elections saw mixed results, with MORENA and its allies retaining a majority in Congress, but losing some ground in key states and municipalities. These outcomes reflect a divided nation with diverse political views and highlight the importance of political dialogue and consensus-building.

The road to 2024 is paved with both challenges and opportunities. Mexico faces pressing issues such as corruption, crime, economic recovery, and the impact of the COVID-19 pandemic. Additionally, social and environmental concerns demand attention, as well as strengthening democratic institutions and safeguarding human rights.

The transition to democracy in Mexico has been a complex and ongoing process, reshaping the nation's political landscape. As the year 2024 approaches, the vision of "The New Power" awaits realization. This chapter offers an exploration of the democratic journey, from the challenges and triumphs of the past to the complexities and aspirations that shape the current political landscape. As Mexico moves forward, it is in the hands of its citizens, political leaders, and civil society to forge a path towards a more inclusive, prosperous, and democratic future.

POLITICAL INSTITUTIONS AND GOVERNANCE

THE PRESIDENCY AND EXECUTIVE POWER

At the helm of Mexico's political machinery stands the presidency, wielding immense executive power and shouldering significant responsibilities. The office of the president plays a central role in shaping the nation's policies, governance, and international relations. This chapter delves into the historical evolution of the presidency, explores the constitutional powers vested in the office, and examines the role of the president in the contemporary political landscape as Mexico approaches the year 2024.

The Evolution of the Mexican Presidency

The roots of the Mexican presidency can be traced back to the country's struggle for independence and the establishment of its first republican government. Early presidents, such as Guadalupe Victoria and Vicente Guerrero, grappled with the challenges of nation-building and forging a unified identity after years of colonial rule.

The 19th century saw a series of strong leaders who shaped Mexico's political landscape, from Benito Juárez's efforts to modernize the nation to Porfirio Díaz's long-lasting rule. The Mexican Revolution marked a significant turning point, leading to constitutional reforms that sought to curb executive power and lay the groundwork for a more inclusive and democratic system.

The Mexican Presidency in the 20th Century

In the post-revolutionary period, the presidency assumed a prominent role in Mexican politics, with a tradition of dominant party rule by the Institutional Revolutionary Party (PRI). Presidents during this era, such as Lázaro Cárdenas and Luis Echeverría, played instrumental roles in advancing social and economic reforms. However, concentration of power and control under the PRI also gave rise to concerns over accountability and democratic governance.

The transition to multi-party politics in the late 20th century brought greater pluralism, competition, and checks on executive power. Presidents from opposition parties, such as Vicente Fox and Felipe Calderón of the National Action Party (PAN), sought to diversify the political landscape, emphasizing economic liberalization and security.

The AMLO Presidency: A New Chapter

In 2018, Andrés Manuel López Obrador (AMLO) was elected as Mexico's president, marking a significant shift in the country's political landscape. As the first left-wing president in recent Mexican history, AMLO's presidency represents a departure from previous administrations. He promised transformative change, emphasizing social justice, anti-corruption measures, and economic policies aimed at addressing inequalities.

AMLO's administration has taken a more interventionist approach, asserting state control over key sectors, such as energy and education, while also advocating for fiscal discipline and reducing bureaucratic inefficiencies. However, his presidency has faced criticisms from some quarters over concerns about centralization of power, disregard for institutional checks and balances, and policy decisions that have raised uncertainty among investors.

The Constitutional Powers of the President

The Mexican Constitution grants the president vast executive powers. The president serves as the head of state and government, responsible for formulating and executing national policies. The officeholder has the authority to appoint and remove cabinet members, shape foreign policy, propose legislation, and issue executive decrees. Additionally, the president is the commander-in-chief of the armed forces, entrusted with ensuring national security and protecting Mexico's territorial integrity.

Challenges and Opportunities

As Mexico approaches the year 2024, the presidency faces a range of challenges and opportunities. Issues such as corruption, crime, economic recovery, social inequality, and environmental sustainability demand effective leadership and policy solutions. Balancing the need for strong executive action with respect for democratic principles and the rule of law remains a delicate task for the president.

The Mexican presidency is a key pillar of the nation's political system, wielding significant influence over policies and governance. From its historical evolution to the powers vested in the office, this chapter has provided an overview of the presidency's role in shaping Mexico's political landscape. As "The New Power" era unfolds in Mexico, the presidency's exercise of executive power will be instrumental in navigating the challenges and shaping the nation's future trajectory.

ROLE OF THE PRESIDENT IN MEXICAN POLITICS

The presidency occupies a pivotal position in Mexican politics, serving as the fulcrum of executive power and national leadership. As Mexico approaches the year 2024, the role of the president continues to be a focal point of public attention and debate. This chapter delves into the multifaceted role of the president, examining their powers, responsibilities, and influence on policymaking, governance, and national development. Additionally, we explore the challenges and opportunities faced by the president in a dynamic political landscape characterized by demands for transformative change and inclusive governance.

Head of State and Symbol of Unity

The president of Mexico is not only the chief executive but also the head of state, embodying the nation's unity and identity. The president represents the country both domestically and internationally, engaging in diplomatic relations with foreign nations and projecting Mexico's image on the global stage. Ceremonial functions, state visits, and national events are all part of the president's role as a unifying figure, bringing diverse segments of Mexican society together under a common banner.

Chief Executive and Policy Formulator

As the chief executive, the president exercises significant powers in the formulation and implementation of national policies. They are responsible for setting the agenda and priorities of the government, shaping the direction of the country's development, and addressing pressing challenges. The president oversees government ministries and agencies, appoints cabinet members, and plays a crucial role in crafting legislation and executive orders that have far-reaching implications for the nation.

Commander-in-Chief of the Armed Forces

One of the most crucial roles of the president is serving as the commander-in-chief of the Mexican armed forces. The president is entrusted with safeguarding the nation's security and territorial integrity. They must make critical decisions related to national defense, combating internal and external threats, and maintaining the country's sovereignty. The role of the president as commander-in-chief necessitates a delicate balance between security imperatives and respect for human rights and the rule of law.

Foreign Policy and International Relations

The president plays a leading role in shaping Mexico's foreign policy and engaging with the international community. Building diplomatic alliances, fostering economic partnerships, and promoting Mexican interests globally are integral components of the president's responsibilities. Key international issues, such as trade agreements, immigration, and climate change, require astute diplomatic acumen and strategic decision-making on the part of the president.

Leadership in Times of Crisis and Uncertainty

During times of crisis, the president's leadership comes under intense scrutiny. Natural disasters, economic downturns, and health emergencies demand swift and effective responses from the government. The president's ability to rally the nation, demonstrate empathy, and offer coherent solutions can significantly influence public perceptions and national unity in the face of adversity.

Challenges and Opportunities

The role of the president in Mexican politics comes with its fair share of challenges and opportunities. Striking a balance between executive authority and respect for democratic principles is a delicate task. The concentration of power in the presidency can lead to concerns about accountability and checks on executive actions. Additionally, the political landscape often requires the president to navigate through a diverse array of interest groups, political parties, and societal demands.

Furthermore, the president must confront various policy challenges, such as combating corruption, addressing social inequalities, promoting economic growth, and ensuring sustainable development. Engaging in meaningful dialogue with stakeholders, including civil society organizations and the private sector, is essential for inclusive governance and effective policy outcomes.

The role of the president in Mexican politics is multi-dimensional and dynamic, encompassing responsibilities as head of state, chief executive, and commander-in-chief. As Mexico stands at the cusp of the "The New Power" era in 2024, the leadership of the president will play a pivotal role in shaping the nation's trajectory. Effective governance, prudent decision-making, and an unwavering commitment to democratic principles will be crucial in addressing challenges and unlocking the vast potential of Mexico's future.

ANALYSIS OF CURRENT PRESIDENTIAL ADMINISTRATION

As Mexico approaches the year 2024, the nation finds itself under the leadership of Andrés Manuel López Obrador (AMLO), who assumed office as president in 2018. AMLO's presidency represents a significant departure from previous administrations, as he leads the country with a vision of transformative change and social justice. This chapter provides an in-depth analysis of the current presidential administration, examining its key policies, achievements, challenges, and the impact of its governance on Mexico's political and social landscape.

AMLO's Vision for "The Fourth Transformation"

From the outset, AMLO's administration pledged to bring about a "Fourth Transformation" of Mexico, a reference to three previous transformative periods in the country's history - the War of Independence, the Reform Laws, and the Mexican Revolution. AMLO's vision revolves around combatting corruption, addressing social inequalities, promoting national self-sufficiency, and prioritizing the needs of the poor and marginalized.

Social Welfare and Anti-Poverty Programs

A hallmark of AMLO's presidency has been the emphasis on social welfare programs. Initiatives such as "Sembrando Vida" (Sowing Life) provide financial support and training to rural farmers, while "Jóvenes Construyendo el Futuro" (Youth Building the Future) aims to empower young people by providing education and work opportunities. While these programs have been praised for their potential to alleviate poverty, critics have raised concerns about long-term sustainability and the risk of creating dependency on government support.

Infrastructure and Development Projects

AMLO's administration has placed significant emphasis on infrastructure development, aiming to bolster economic growth and regional connectivity. Projects such as the Maya Train and the Dos Bocas oil refinery have been key priorities. Proponents argue that these projects will stimulate the economy and create jobs, especially in underdeveloped regions. However, critics raise environmental and financial sustainability concerns, questioning the long-term benefits of these initiatives.

Security and Crime

Addressing the issue of crime and violence remains a major challenge for the current administration. Despite efforts to establish the National Guard as a central pillar of security strategy, Mexico continues to grapple with drug-related violence, organized crime, and human rights abuses. The president's stance on deploying the military for public security duties has sparked debate over the balance between security imperatives and respect for human rights.

Energy Policy and Sovereignty

Energy policy has been a contentious issue under AMLO's administration. He has sought to strengthen state control over the energy sector, particularly by supporting the state-owned oil company, Pemex. This has included limiting private sector involvement and rolling back previous energy reforms. While some view this as a move towards energy sovereignty and protection of national resources, others argue that it hinders investment and innovation in the sector.

Relationship with Media and Critics

The president's combative relationship with the media and critics has been a recurring theme during his tenure. AMLO has frequently dismissed critical reporting as "fake news" and has opted for direct communication with the public through daily press conferences. This approach has raised concerns about media freedom and the role of independent journalism in holding the government accountable.

The current presidential administration under Andrés Manuel López Obrador has brought a distinct vision of change and social welfare to Mexico's political landscape. With an emphasis on addressing social inequalities, combatting corruption, and advancing national sovereignty, AMLO's presidency has generated passionate support and opposition. As Mexico approaches the year 2024, the impact of the administration's policies and governance on the nation's development and political direction will continue to shape the course of "The New Power" era in Mexico. The ongoing challenges and opportunities faced by the administration will influence the narrative of Mexico's future and the pursuit of its transformative goals.

CONGRESS AND THE LEGISLATIVE PROCESS

In Mexico's democratic system, the Congress plays a vital role as the legislative branch of government. Comprising the Chamber of Deputies and the Senate, Congress holds the power to enact laws, oversee the executive branch, and represent the diverse interests of the Mexican people. As "The New Power" era approaches in 2024, the functioning and dynamics of Congress become paramount in shaping the nation's policies and governance. This chapter delves into the structure, functions, and significance of Congress in Mexican politics, as well as its role in driving legislative initiatives and ensuring democratic accountability.

The Structure of Mexican Congress

The Mexican Congress consists of two chambers: the Chamber of Deputies and the Senate. The Chamber of Deputies is composed of 500 members elected through a mixed system of single-member districts and proportional representation. The Senate, on the other hand, comprises 128 members, two for each state and the Federal District (now Mexico City), elected for six-year terms. The proportional representation aspect ensures a degree of pluralism, allowing for representation of multiple political parties and diverse viewpoints.

Functions and Powers of Congress

Congress holds several essential functions and powers in Mexico's political system. Its primary role is to legislate, debating, and passing laws that govern the country. This includes laws related to the economy, education, security, social welfare, and more. Congress also exercises oversight over the executive branch, scrutinizing the president's actions, budgetary allocation, and administrative decisions.

Additionally, Congress has the power to approve international treaties and agreements negotiated by the executive branch, ensuring that they align with Mexico's national interests. Furthermore, the Constitution grants Congress the authority to amend the fundamental law, although some amendments require approval by a majority of the state legislatures.

The Legislative Process

The legislative process in Mexico involves multiple stages. A bill may originate in either chamber, and it goes through several readings, committee discussions, and debates before becoming law. In the case of significant reforms, both chambers must approve the bill before it is sent to the president for promulgation.

The committees play a crucial role in scrutinizing proposed legislation, conducting in-depth analyses, and making recommendations for amendments. Public consultations and expert testimonies are sometimes held to gather input from civil society and stakeholders.

The Role of Political Parties

Political parties play a central role in Congress, as their representation shapes the legislative landscape. The majority party holds significant influence, often determining which bills are prioritized and the direction of the legislative agenda. Coalition-building is common in Mexican politics, with parties forming alliances to achieve their policy objectives.

Challenges and Opportunities

Congress faces various challenges in fulfilling its functions effectively. Party discipline and political polarization can sometimes hinder constructive debate and consensus-building. Moreover, ensuring transparent and accountable governance remains an ongoing challenge.

However, Congress also presents opportunities for meaningful change and progress. As diverse voices from different political parties and backgrounds converge, the potential for inclusive policymaking and representation of various interests is significant. The role of civil society in engaging with Congress, voicing concerns, and advocating for specific policy issues can foster greater accountability and responsiveness from lawmakers.

The Mexican Congress stands as a vital institution in the nation's democratic governance, representing the interests of the people and shaping the legal framework that governs the country. As Mexico moves towards "The New Power" era in 2024, Congress will continue to play a critical role in shaping policies and ensuring checks and balances within the political system. By fostering dialogue, cooperation, and inclusive decision-making, Congress can uphold democratic values and contribute to the nation's advancement in the years to come.

STRUCTURE AND FUNCTIONS OF THE MEXICAN CONGRESS

In the Mexican political landscape, the Congress stands as a pivotal institution, embodying the democratic principles of representation, legislation, and oversight. Comprising the Chamber of Deputies and the Senate, the Mexican Congress plays a central role in shaping the nation's laws, policies, and governance. This chapter delves into the structure, functions, and significance of the Mexican Congress, highlighting its role in driving legislative initiatives and ensuring democratic accountability in the "New Power" era of Mexico.

The Bicameral Legislature

The Mexican Congress operates under a bicameral system, consisting of two chambers: the Chamber of Deputies and the Senate. This setup ensures a balance of representation and allows for more comprehensive legislative scrutiny. While both chambers participate in the lawmaking process, they have distinct roles and functions.

The Chamber of Deputies

The Chamber of Deputies is the lower house of Congress, consisting of 500 members, or deputies, who represent single-member districts and are elected for three-year terms. The size of the Chamber allows for a proportional representation of the population, giving a voice to diverse regions and constituencies across Mexico.

The Senate

The Senate, as the upper house, is composed of 128 members, two for each state and the Federal District (now Mexico City). Senators serve six-year terms, with half of the seats up for election every three years. This staggered election system helps maintain continuity and ensures that the Senate is not subject to sudden shifts in political power.

Functions and Powers of the Mexican Congress

The Mexican Congress holds several key functions and powers essential to the functioning of the country's democratic system:

Legislation: Congress is responsible for proposing, debating, and passing laws that govern various aspects of Mexican society, including economic policies, social welfare, education, security, and more. Proposed bills can originate in either chamber and must go through multiple readings and committee reviews before becoming law.

Oversight: Congress plays a crucial role in overseeing the actions of the executive branch, including the president and cabinet members. This oversight function involves scrutinizing government policies, budget allocation, and administrative decisions to ensure accountability and transparency.

Budgetary Authority: Congress holds the power of the purse, with the authority to approve the federal budget proposed by the executive branch. This includes determining allocations for various government programs and public initiatives.

Ratification of International Treaties: The Senate has the responsibility to approve or reject international treaties and agreements negotiated by the executive branch. This ensures that Mexico's foreign policy aligns with its national interests and values.

Constitutional Amendments: Congress has the authority to amend the Constitution, although some amendments require the approval of a majority of state legislatures. Constitutional amendments are significant as they shape the fundamental principles and structure of the Mexican government.

The Legislative Process

The legislative process in the Mexican Congress involves multiple stages, promoting thorough deliberation and public participation. A proposed bill may originate in either chamber, and it goes through readings, committee discussions, and debates. Public consultations and expert testimonies are occasionally conducted to gather input from civil society and stakeholders.

Party Dynamics and Coalition Building

Political parties play a crucial role in Congress, and the majority party often determines the legislative agenda and priorities. In the Mexican political landscape, coalition-building is common, as parties form alliances to advance their policy objectives and secure support for legislation.

The Mexican Congress, with its bicameral structure and array of functions, plays a central role in shaping the nation's laws and policies. As Mexico moves into "The New Power" era in 2024, the Congress will continue to be a vital institution, representing the diverse interests of the Mexican people and ensuring democratic governance and accountability. By fostering dialogue, cooperation, and inclusive decision-making, the Congress can contribute to the nation's advancement and address the challenges and opportunities of a rapidly changing political landscape.

KEY LEGISLATIVE INITIATIVES AND CHALLENGES

As Mexico ventures into "The New Power" era in 2024, the Mexican Congress faces a myriad of legislative initiatives and challenges that will shape the nation's political landscape and governance. This chapter explores some of the key legislative priorities that the Congress is likely to address in the coming years. It also highlights the challenges that lawmakers will encounter in advancing these initiatives while ensuring inclusivity, transparency, and responsiveness to the diverse needs of the Mexican people.

Economic Recovery and Growth

One of the primary objectives of the Mexican Congress will be to enact legislation aimed at fostering economic recovery and sustainable growth. Measures to attract foreign investment, stimulate domestic industries, and create job opportunities will be paramount to address the economic impacts of the COVID-19 pandemic and advance the nation's development.

Social Welfare and Poverty Alleviation

In line with the vision of "The Fourth Transformation," Congress will continue to focus on social welfare programs aimed at reducing poverty and inequality. Improving access to education, healthcare, and affordable housing will be critical components of the legislative agenda to uplift the most vulnerable segments of society.

Security and Crime

The Congress will grapple with the challenge of enhancing security measures to combat organized crime and violence effectively. Legislation aimed at bolstering law enforcement, improving intelligence gathering, and addressing root causes of crime will be crucial in ensuring citizen safety and the rule of law.

Environmental Sustainability

Addressing environmental challenges will be a pressing legislative priority. Congress must devise policies to mitigate climate change, preserve natural resources, and promote sustainable development. Legislation supporting clean energy initiatives and responsible land use will be instrumental in safeguarding Mexico's environment for future generations.

Healthcare Reform

The pandemic has underscored the importance of a robust and accessible healthcare system. The Congress will explore healthcare reforms to strengthen the public health infrastructure, expand coverage, and ensure healthcare services reach all corners of the nation.

Energy Policy and Sovereignty

Energy policy will continue to be a contested issue in the Mexican Congress. Striking a balance between energy sovereignty and attracting private investment will be a key challenge. Addressing concerns related to Pemex's financial stability and promoting renewable energy sources will be central to the legislative debate.

Political and Electoral Reforms

Advancing political and electoral reforms will be critical to strengthen democratic institutions and ensure free and fair elections. The Congress may consider initiatives to enhance campaign finance transparency, promote voter participation, and foster a level playing field for political parties.

Human Rights and Social Justice

Promoting human rights and social justice will be a fundamental aspect of the legislative agenda. Addressing issues such as gender equality, LGBTQ+ rights, and indigenous rights will require comprehensive legislation that ensures equal protection and opportunities for all.

Challenges

While addressing these legislative initiatives, the Mexican Congress will face various challenges:

Political Polarization: Political polarization may hinder constructive dialogue and compromise, making it challenging to build consensus around critical issues.

Fiscal Constraints: Implementing ambitious policies will require addressing fiscal constraints and balancing social spending with sustainable economic growth.

Public Participation: Ensuring meaningful public participation in the legislative process and incorporating diverse perspectives will be essential for inclusive governance.

Lobbying and Interest Groups: Managing the influence of interest groups and lobbying efforts on legislative decisions will be crucial to preserving the integrity of the democratic process.

The Mexican Congress will be at the forefront of shaping Mexico's trajectory in "The New Power" era. By tackling key legislative initiatives and addressing challenges head-on, lawmakers have the opportunity to drive transformative change, foster sustainable development, and ensure the welfare of all citizens. Upholding democratic principles, transparency, and accountability will be paramount as the Congress navigates the complexities of Mexican politics to advance the nation's aspirations and aspirations.

THE JUDICIARY AND RULE OF LAW

In any democratic society, the judiciary plays a pivotal role in upholding the rule of law and safeguarding the principles of justice and fairness. As Mexico approaches "The New Power" era in 2024, the independence and effectiveness of the judiciary become even more crucial in ensuring democratic stability and protecting the rights and liberties of its citizens. This chapter delves into the structure and functions of the Mexican judiciary, the challenges it faces, and its significance in promoting the rule of law and fostering a just and equitable society.

The Structure of the Mexican Judiciary

The Mexican judiciary is organized into a hierarchical structure that spans federal and state levels. At the federal level, the judiciary comprises the Supreme Court of Justice of the Nation (Suprema Corte de Justicia de la Nación) and various circuit and district courts. State-level judiciaries are responsible for administering justice within their respective states.

The Supreme Court of Justice of the Nation

The Supreme Court is the highest judicial authority in Mexico. It is composed of eleven justices, known as ministers, who are appointed by the president and confirmed by the Senate. The Court has the power to interpret the Constitution, resolve conflicts between federal entities and states, and ensure uniformity in the application of the law throughout the country.

Functions of the Mexican Judiciary

The judiciary's primary function is to interpret and apply the law in a fair and impartial manner. Its role extends beyond settling disputes; it also serves as a check on the executive and legislative branches, ensuring that their actions align with constitutional principles and respect human rights.

The Mexican judiciary is responsible for adjudicating both civil and criminal cases, including those involving constitutional matters, administrative disputes, and electoral issues. Its decisions set legal precedents and establish the jurisprudence that guides the country's legal framework.

The Independence of the Judiciary

Judicial independence is fundamental to the judiciary's effectiveness and its ability to act as a check on other branches of government. An independent judiciary is free from external influence and political pressure, allowing it to make impartial decisions based on the law and evidence presented in court.

The Rule of Law and Its Importance

The rule of law is a cornerstone of any democratic society, ensuring that laws are applied equally to all individuals and institutions, regardless of their status or power. Upholding the rule of law guarantees the protection of human rights, due process, and a fair and just legal system.

Challenges to the Judiciary

Despite its crucial role, the Mexican judiciary faces several challenges:

Corruption: Corruption remains a significant concern within the judicial system, with some judges and court officials susceptible to external influence or bribery. Addressing corruption is essential for restoring public trust in the judiciary.

Backlog of Cases: The judiciary grapples with a backlog of cases, leading to delays in the administration of justice. Implementing measures to expedite proceedings and enhance court efficiency is vital.

Security Concerns: Judges, lawyers, and witnesses face security threats, particularly in areas affected by organized crime. Ensuring the safety of those involved in legal proceedings is essential for the rule of law to prevail.

Access to Justice: Ensuring equitable access to justice for all citizens, regardless of socioeconomic background, is a challenge. Promoting legal aid services and enhancing judicial accessibility can help address this issue.

In the pursuit of "The New Power" in Mexico, a strong, independent, and effective judiciary is paramount. Upholding the rule of law and ensuring equal access to justice will be instrumental in promoting democratic stability, protecting human rights, and fostering a just and equitable society. By addressing the challenges facing the judiciary and upholding the principles of fairness and impartiality, Mexico can strengthen its legal institutions and lay the foundation for a more prosperous and inclusive future.

THE INDEPENDENCE OF THE JUDICIARY AND ITS IMPORTANCE

In any democratic society, the independence of the judiciary is a cornerstone of the rule of law and a fundamental pillar of a just and equitable legal system. As Mexico approaches "The New Power" era in 2024, understanding and upholding the independence of the judiciary become critical in safeguarding democratic principles, protecting human rights, and ensuring the effective functioning of the country's legal institutions. This chapter explores the significance of an independent judiciary, the challenges it faces, and the impact of judicial independence on Mexico's political and social landscape.

The Concept of Judicial Independence

Judicial independence refers to the principle that the judiciary operates free from undue influence or interference from external actors, such as the executive or legislative branches of government, private interests, or political pressure. It allows judges to make impartial decisions based solely on the law and the evidence presented in court.

The Importance of an Independent Judiciary

An independent judiciary is vital for several reasons:

Rule of Law: Judicial independence upholds the rule of law, ensuring that laws are applied consistently and equally to all individuals and institutions. It prevents the arbitrary exercise of power and ensures legal certainty and predictability.

Protection of Human Rights: An independent judiciary acts as a safeguard against violations of human rights. It can hold government authorities accountable for abuses and protect the rights and liberties of individuals, particularly vulnerable and marginalized populations.

Checks and Balances: An independent judiciary acts as a check on the executive and legislative branches, ensuring that their actions conform to the Constitution and respect the division of powers.

Impartial Adjudication: Judges' independence allows them to decide cases based on the merits and the law, free from personal bias, political pressure, or external influences. This ensures a fair and just legal process.

Public Confidence: An independent judiciary inspires public confidence in the legal system. When people believe that judges are fair and impartial, they are more likely to respect and abide by the law.

Economic Development: A stable and independent judiciary is essential for attracting foreign investment and promoting economic growth. Investors need confidence that their rights will be protected under the law.

Challenges to Judicial Independence

While judicial independence is crucial, it faces several challenges:

Political Interference: Political pressure from the executive or legislative branches can undermine judicial independence and compromise the impartiality of judges.

Corruption: Corruption within the judiciary can erode public trust and confidence in the legal system. It is essential to address and root out corruption to ensure an independent judiciary.

Insufficient Resources: Inadequate funding and resources can hamper the judiciary's ability to function effectively, leading to delays in legal proceedings.

Security Concerns: Judges and court personnel may face security threats, particularly in regions affected by organized crime or political violence.

Promoting Judicial Independence

To promote and uphold judicial independence, several measures can be taken:

Secure Tenure: Ensuring judges have secure tenure and protection against arbitrary removal safeguards them from political interference.

Transparent Selection Process: Implementing a transparent and merit-based process for appointing judges can enhance the perception of fairness and impartiality.

Adequate Funding: Providing sufficient resources and funding to the judiciary is essential for its effective functioning.

Judicial Training: Continuous professional development and training for judges can enhance their skills and knowledge, leading to better decision-making.

An independent judiciary is the bedrock of a strong and thriving democracy. As Mexico ventures into "The New Power" era in 2024, the promotion and protection of judicial independence will be essential to uphold the rule of law, protect human rights, and foster public trust in the legal system. By addressing challenges and ensuring an impartial and independent judiciary, Mexico can pave the way for a more just, equitable, and prosperous future for all its citizens.

LANDMARK LEGAL CASES SHAPING POLITICS AND SOCIETY

Throughout Mexico's history, certain landmark legal cases have played pivotal roles in shaping the nation's politics and society. These cases have had far-reaching implications, influencing public discourse, political decision-making, and the protection of human rights. As "The New Power" era approaches in 2024, understanding the significance of these landmark legal cases becomes crucial in comprehending Mexico's journey toward democracy, justice, and social progress. This chapter explores some of the most influential legal cases that have left a lasting impact on Mexico's political and social landscape.

Marbury v. Madison (1824)

Although not a Mexican case, the U.S. Supreme Court's ruling in Marbury v. Madison profoundly influenced Mexico's legal and political thinking. The principle of judicial review, established in this case, allowed courts to review the constitutionality of legislative and executive actions. This concept later found its way into Mexico's legal system, influencing the development of judicial independence and constitutionalism.

The Lerdo Law (1856)

The Lerdo Law was a landmark legal initiative that aimed to address land reform in Mexico. It sought to expropriate the property of the Catholic Church and indigenous communities, redistributing the land to peasants. While the law contributed to secularization and land redistribution, it also faced significant opposition and sparked tensions between the Church and the government.

The Juarez Law (1855-1857)

Named after President Benito Juarez, the Juarez Law aimed to separate church and state, nationalize church properties, and limit the Church's influence in politics. It significantly impacted Mexico's political landscape, enshrining secularism as a fundamental principle in the country's Constitution.

The Amparo (Writ of Amparo)

The Amparo is a constitutional remedy that protects individuals' constitutional rights from violations by authorities. It has been instrumental in safeguarding human rights and holding government actions accountable. The Amparo has played a crucial role in protecting freedoms, challenging abusive state practices, and advancing justice in Mexico.

Women's Suffrage (1953)

The legal recognition of women's right to vote in municipal elections in 1953 marked a significant step toward gender equality in Mexico. Subsequently, in 1958, women gained the right to vote in federal elections. These landmark cases expanded political representation for women, empowering them to participate in the democratic process.

Zapatistas' Indigenous Rights Case (1994)

The Zapatista uprising in 1994 brought the issue of indigenous rights to the forefront of Mexico's political agenda. The case of the Zapatistas highlighted the historic marginalization and lack of political representation faced by indigenous communities. The movement influenced discussions on autonomy, land rights, and cultural recognition for indigenous populations.

LGBT Rights and Same-Sex Marriage (2015)

In 2015, the Mexican Supreme Court ruled that state bans on same-sex marriage were unconstitutional. The landmark case opened the door to marriage equality across Mexico, granting equal rights and recognition to same-sex couples.

Ayotzinapa Case (2014)

The disappearance of 43 students from the Ayotzinapa Rural Teachers' College in 2014 sparked national outrage and international attention. The case shed light on issues of corruption, violence, and impunity in Mexico, leading to widespread demands for justice and accountability.

Landmark legal cases have left an indelible mark on Mexico's politics and society, shaping the nation's trajectory toward democracy, justice, and human rights. As Mexico approaches "The New Power" era in 2024, these cases serve as reminders of the importance of upholding the rule of law, promoting equality, and protecting the rights of all citizens. By learning from the past and addressing ongoing challenges, Mexico can continue its journey toward a more just, inclusive, and democratic society.

ADDRESSING SOCIETAL CHALLENGES

COMBATING CORRUPTION AND ENSURING TRANSPARENCY

Corruption has long been a pervasive issue in Mexican politics, hindering development, eroding public trust, and impeding progress. As Mexico enters "The New Power" era in 2024, the fight against corruption and the pursuit of transparency become critical elements in shaping the nation's political landscape. This chapter delves into the challenges posed by corruption, the importance of transparency in governance, and the strategies and initiatives required to combat corruption effectively and foster a culture of transparency in Mexico's political sphere.

The Impact of Corruption on Politics and Society

Corruption exerts a profound impact on Mexico's politics and society, affecting various aspects of governance and public life:

Erosion of Public Trust: Widespread corruption erodes public trust in government institutions and politicians. Citizens become disillusioned and cynical about the effectiveness of public policies and their representatives.

Diversion of Public Funds: Corruption siphons public funds away from essential services, such as healthcare, education, and infrastructure, depriving citizens of much-needed resources.

Impediment to Economic Growth: Corruption discourages foreign investment and hinders economic growth, as investors seek stable and transparent environments.

Social Inequity: Corruption exacerbates social inequalities by favoring well-connected individuals or corporations over the broader population.

Undermining the Rule of Law: Corruption weakens the rule of law, as powerful individuals evade accountability and legal consequences.

Transparency as an Antidote to Corruption

Transparency serves as a powerful tool in combating corruption and promoting good governance:

Accountability: Transparency fosters accountability by making government actions, decisions, and expenditures visible to the public.

Citizen Engagement: Transparent governance encourages citizen participation, empowering individuals to demand accountability and participate in decision-making.

Anti-Corruption Measures: Transparent processes, such as procurement and public contracts, can minimize opportunities for corruption.

Public Trust and Legitimacy: Transparent governance builds public trust and legitimacy in government institutions.

Reducing Information Asymmetry: Transparency reduces information asymmetry between the government and citizens, ensuring access to vital information.

Challenges in Combating Corruption

Combating corruption requires addressing various challenges:

Deep-Rooted Culture: Corruption is deeply entrenched in Mexican political culture, necessitating a cultural shift towards transparency and accountability.

Weak Institutions: Strengthening institutions is crucial to ensure effective oversight and enforcement of anti-corruption measures.

Political Will: Political will is essential to initiate and sustain anti-corruption reforms, even in the face of vested interests.

Judicial Independence: A robust, independent judiciary is crucial to prosecuting corrupt individuals impartially.

Collaboration and International Cooperation: Combating corruption often requires international collaboration to address cross-border issues and illicit financial flows.

Strategies for Transparency and Anti-Corruption

To foster transparency and combat corruption effectively, Mexico can consider several strategies:

Whistleblower Protection: Strengthening whistleblower protection laws encourages individuals to report corruption without fear of reprisal.

Asset Declarations: Requiring public officials to declare their assets can help identify suspicious wealth accumulation.

Open Data and Technology: Utilizing technology to publish government data and information in an accessible format enhances transparency.

Strengthening Independent Oversight Bodies: Empowering institutions such as the Ombudsman and anti-corruption commissions bolsters accountability.

Public Awareness Campaigns: Engaging citizens through public awareness campaigns raises consciousness about the impact of corruption and the importance of transparency.

Combating corruption and promoting transparency are central to Mexico's journey toward "The New Power" in 2024. By upholding transparency, fostering accountability, and strengthening institutions, Mexico can address the challenges posed by corruption and pave the way for a more just, equitable, and democratic society. A commitment to transparency and anti-corruption measures will be instrumental in building public trust, attracting investment, and ensuring sustainable development in Mexico's political landscape.

CORRUPTION AS A POLITICAL ISSUE

Corruption has emerged as a deeply entrenched and pervasive issue in Mexican politics, profoundly shaping the nation's political landscape and public perception. As Mexico embarks on "The New Power" era in 2024, addressing corruption as a central political issue becomes imperative in restoring public trust, promoting good governance, and fostering a more transparent and accountable political system. This chapter examines corruption as a political issue, its causes and consequences, and the strategies and initiatives required to combat corruption effectively in Mexico.

Corruption in Mexican Politics

Corruption has become synonymous with Mexican politics, impacting various aspects of governance and political processes:

Patronage Politics: Corruption thrives in a system characterized by patronage and clientelism, where political favors are exchanged for loyalty and support.

Influence of Organized Crime: The influence of organized crime in politics and government institutions exacerbates corruption, making it difficult to prosecute and hold accountable those involved.

Impunity: The lack of accountability and impunity for corrupt acts allows corrupt officials to act without fear of consequences.

Political Financing: Illicit campaign financing and lack of transparency in political donations create opportunities for corruption and undue influence.

Collusion Between Public and Private Sectors: Collusion between public officials and private entities fosters corrupt practices, such as bribery, kickbacks, and embezzlement.

Consequences of Corruption

The consequences of corruption are far-reaching and detrimental to Mexico's political and social fabric:

Erosion of Public Trust: Corruption erodes public trust in government institutions and political leaders, undermining democratic legitimacy.

Economic Impact: Corruption diverts public funds, hinders economic growth, and deters foreign investment.

Social Inequity: Corruption perpetuates social inequalities, as resources meant for public welfare are misappropriated for personal gain.

Undermining Rule of Law: Corruption weakens the rule of law, as powerful individuals manipulate legal processes for their benefit.

Weakening Institutions: Corrupt practices weaken the effectiveness and credibility of public institutions.

Strategies to Address Corruption

Addressing corruption as a political issue requires comprehensive strategies and initiatives:

Transparency and Accountability: Promoting transparency in government processes, finances, and decision-making enhances accountability and reduces opportunities for corruption.

Independent Oversight: Strengthening independent oversight bodies and anti-corruption institutions ensures effective monitoring and enforcement of anti-corruption measures.

Whistleblower Protection: Providing robust protection to whistleblowers encourages reporting of corrupt practices without fear of retaliation.

Campaign Finance Reform: Implementing campaign finance reform ensures transparency and accountability in political donations and expenditures.

Judicial Independence: Fostering an independent and impartial judiciary is vital for prosecuting corrupt officials and upholding the rule of law.

Education and Public Awareness: Raising public awareness about the impact of corruption and promoting ethical behavior fosters a culture of integrity.

Corruption as a political issue is a formidable challenge facing Mexico as it moves into "The New Power" era in 2024. By prioritizing transparency, accountability, and anti-corruption measures, Mexico can work toward restoring public trust in its political institutions and leaders. Addressing corruption requires a collective effort from all sectors of society, fostering a commitment to good governance, integrity, and the principles of democracy. A resolute focus on combating corruption will be instrumental in shaping Mexico's political future and ensuring a more just, transparent, and accountable political landscape.

ANTI-CORRUPTION EFFORTS AND THEIR IMPACT

In the pursuit of "The New Power" in Mexico, combatting corruption stands as a paramount objective to foster good governance, restore public trust, and promote transparency. Over the years, various anti-corruption efforts have been implemented to address this pervasive issue. This chapter explores the impact of anti-corruption initiatives in Mexico, examining the progress made, the challenges faced, and the path forward to strengthen these efforts and achieve tangible results in the years leading up to 2024.

Historical Context of Anti-Corruption Efforts

Mexico's anti-corruption efforts have evolved over time, responding to changing political dynamics and societal demands:

Establishment of Anti-Corruption Institutions: Institutions like the Secretariat of Public Administration (SFP) and the Federal Institute for Access to Information and Data Protection (IFAI) were created to monitor and enforce anti-corruption measures.

The National Anti-Corruption System (SNA): The SNA, established in 2016, aimed to coordinate efforts across all levels of government to combat corruption, enhance transparency, and ensure accountability.

Whistleblower Protection Laws: Legislation to protect whistleblowers has been enacted to encourage reporting of corrupt practices and protect those who come forward.

International Cooperation: Mexico has engaged in international collaboration to address corruption, working with organizations like the United Nations and the Organization for Economic Cooperation and Development (OECD).

Impact of Anti-Corruption Efforts

The impact of anti-corruption efforts in Mexico has been multifaceted:

Increased Public Awareness: Anti-corruption initiatives have raised public awareness about the detrimental effects of corruption and the need for transparency and accountability.

Whistleblower Reports: The protection of whistleblowers has led to an increase in reports of corruption, enabling authorities to uncover and investigate corrupt practices.

High-Profile Cases: Notable cases involving corrupt officials and politicians have been brought to light, leading to public outrage and demands for accountability.

Strengthened Institutions: Anti-corruption efforts have contributed to the strengthening of anti-corruption institutions and the establishment of the SNA.

Challenges and Limitations

Despite progress, anti-corruption efforts in Mexico face challenges and limitations:

Impunity and Weak Prosecution: High levels of impunity and weak prosecution of corrupt officials undermine the effectiveness of anti-corruption measures.

Political Will and Interests: The influence of vested interests and political will can hinder the implementation and enforcement of anti-corruption policies.

Inadequate Resources: Insufficient funding and resources may limit the capacity of anti-corruption institutions to carry out their mandate effectively.

Complexity of Corruption Networks: Corruption networks often involve collusion between public and private actors, making investigations and prosecutions intricate and time-consuming.

The Path Forward

To strengthen anti-corruption efforts and achieve significant impact by 2024, Mexico must consider the following measures:

Judicial Independence: Ensuring an independent and impartial judiciary is vital to prosecuting corrupt officials and increasing public trust in the legal system.

Comprehensive Reforms: Implementing comprehensive reforms that address the root causes of corruption, such as campaign finance, public procurement, and government contracting.

Whistleblower Protection: Enhancing whistleblower protection mechanisms to encourage reporting and protect those who expose corruption.

International Collaboration: Strengthening international cooperation and engaging with international organizations to address cross-border corruption issues.

Civil Society Engagement: Encouraging active participation and collaboration with civil society organizations to foster transparency and hold authorities accountable.

The impact of anti-corruption efforts in Mexico will be instrumental in shaping the nation's political landscape in "The New Power" era of 2024. By building on progress made, addressing challenges, and pursuing comprehensive reforms, Mexico can forge a path toward a more transparent, accountable, and corruption-free political system. The commitment to combating corruption must remain a top priority, engaging all sectors of society in a collective effort to achieve lasting change and uphold the principles of good governance and integrity.

TACKLING CRIME AND ENHANCING SECURITY

Crime and security issues have long been a major concern in Mexico's political landscape, impacting public safety, economic development, and social stability. As Mexico approaches "The New Power" era in 2024, addressing crime and enhancing security becomes paramount to foster a safer and more prosperous nation. This chapter delves into the challenges posed by crime, the strategies to tackle criminal activities, and the initiatives required to enhance security and create a more secure environment for all citizens.

Crime Landscape in Mexico

Mexico faces a complex and diverse crime landscape, including:

Organized Crime: Powerful drug cartels and organized criminal groups operate across the country, engaging in drug trafficking, human smuggling, and other illicit activities.

Violent Crimes: Homicides, kidnappings, and extortions pose significant threats to public safety and stability.

Corruption and Impunity: Corruption within law enforcement and judicial institutions hampers the effective prosecution of criminals and undermines public trust.

Cybercrime: The rise of cybercrime presents new challenges in tackling digital fraud, data breaches, and online scams.

Strategies to Tackle Crime

Addressing crime and enhancing security require comprehensive strategies:

Strengthening Law Enforcement: Investing in law enforcement capabilities, training, and equipment to effectively combat criminal organizations and respond to emergencies.

Intelligence and Surveillance: Enhancing intelligence gathering and surveillance capabilities to track criminal activities and disrupt organized crime networks.

Judicial Reforms: Implementing judicial reforms to expedite criminal trials and increase the likelihood of successful prosecutions.

Community Policing: Promoting community-oriented policing strategies to build trust between law enforcement and citizens, fostering cooperation in crime prevention.

Targeted Anti-Crime Initiatives: Implementing targeted initiatives to address specific crime issues, such as human trafficking, cybercrime, and gender-based violence.

Combating Corruption: Rooting out corruption within law enforcement and judicial institutions to ensure a fair and effective criminal justice system.

Enhancing Security Measures

To enhance security and safeguard public safety, Mexico can consider the following measures:

Border Security: Strengthening border security to curb the flow of illegal drugs, weapons, and human trafficking.

Cybersecurity: Investing in cybersecurity infrastructure and capabilities to protect critical systems and combat digital threats.

Social Programs: Implementing social programs and economic opportunities in marginalized communities to address root causes of crime.

Victim Support Services: Enhancing victim support services to provide assistance and protection for those affected by crime.

International Cooperation: Collaborating with neighboring countries and international partners to address cross-border crime and enhance regional security.

Measuring Success and Challenges

Measuring the success of crime prevention and security efforts involves monitoring key indicators, such as crime rates, clearance rates (percentage of cases solved), and public perception of safety. Challenges to addressing crime and enhancing security include:

Resource Constraints: Limited resources may hinder the implementation of comprehensive security measures.

Long-Term Commitment: Sustainable improvements in security require a long-term commitment and coordinated efforts across all levels of government.

Addressing Root Causes: Effectively tackling crime involves addressing socio-economic disparities and providing viable alternatives to criminal activities.

Tackling crime and enhancing security are critical components of "The New Power" era in Mexico. By implementing comprehensive strategies, strengthening law enforcement and judicial institutions, and investing in community-oriented approaches, Mexico can create a safer and more secure environment for its citizens. Collaboration with international partners and a sustained commitment to addressing crime challenges will be essential in achieving lasting progress and fostering a secure and prosperous future for all Mexicans.

MEXICO'S STRUGGLE AGAINST DRUG CARTELS AND CRIME

Mexico's fight against drug cartels and crime has been an ongoing and complex challenge, shaping the nation's politics, security, and social fabric. As Mexico enters "The New Power" era in 2024, comprehending the dynamics of this struggle becomes crucial in developing effective strategies to dismantle criminal organizations, enhance public safety, and forge a path towards a more secure and peaceful society. This chapter delves into Mexico's struggle against drug cartels and crime, the root causes, the impact on society, and the initiatives required to address this pressing issue.

The Rise of Drug Cartels and Organized Crime

The emergence of powerful drug cartels and organized criminal groups in Mexico is the result of various factors:

Geography: Mexico's geographic location between South American drug-producing countries and the United States, the world's largest drug market, has made it a transit hub for illicit drugs.

Historical Context: The liberalization of drug enforcement policies in the 1980s and 1990s led to the expansion of drug production and trafficking networks in Mexico.

Weak Institutions: Corruption within law enforcement, judiciary, and political institutions facilitated the growth and operations of drug cartels.

Socioeconomic Disparities: Marginalized communities with limited economic opportunities have become recruitment grounds for criminal organizations.

Impact on Society

The presence of drug cartels and crime has had far-reaching consequences on Mexican society:

Violence and Insecurity: Mexico's struggle against drug cartels has resulted in a surge of violence, homicides, and disappearances, causing widespread fear and insecurity.

Displacement and Migration: Ongoing violence has displaced communities and contributed to forced migration within and beyond Mexico's borders.

Corruption and Impunity: Corruption within law enforcement and judicial institutions undermines the ability to effectively combat crime and prosecute criminals.

Social Fragmentation: The prevalence of drug cartels has eroded social cohesion, as communities live in fear of retaliation and exploitation.

Economic Impact: Crime hampers economic growth, deters foreign investment, and diverts resources away from productive endeavors.

Initiatives to Tackle Drug Cartels and Crime

To address Mexico's struggle against drug cartels and crime, comprehensive initiatives are necessary:

Security Forces Strengthening: Investing in training, equipment, and resources for law enforcement and security forces to combat criminal organizations effectively.

Intelligence Sharing: Enhancing intelligence sharing and cooperation between different levels of law enforcement agencies to disrupt criminal networks.

Community Engagement: Implementing community policing and social programs to build trust and address the root causes of crime.

Judicial Reforms: Strengthening the judicial system to ensure fair and timely trials and reduce impunity for criminals.

International Cooperation: Collaborating with other countries to address cross-border crime and curb drug trafficking.

Addressing Socioeconomic Disparities: Implementing inclusive economic policies and social programs to provide viable alternatives to criminal activities.

Mexico's struggle against drug cartels and crime remains a significant challenge as it enters "The New Power" era in 2024. By understanding the root causes, investing in security forces, engaging communities, and addressing social inequalities, Mexico can make strides towards dismantling criminal organizations and fostering a more secure and peaceful society. Combating drug cartels and crime requires a collective effort from all sectors of society and sustained commitment from political leaders to achieve tangible progress and create a safer and more prosperous future for all Mexicans.

STRATEGIES FOR IMPROVING PUBLIC SAFETY

Enhancing public safety is a fundamental priority for Mexico as it approaches "The New Power" era in 2024. Addressing crime, violence, and insecurity requires comprehensive strategies that involve law enforcement, communities, and government institutions working collaboratively. This chapter explores the key strategies for improving public safety in Mexico, focusing on preventive measures, community engagement, and strengthening law enforcement capabilities to create a safer and more secure environment for all citizens.

Community-Oriented Policing

Community-oriented policing emphasizes building trust and cooperation between law enforcement agencies and the communities they serve:

Community Engagement: Encouraging police officers to interact positively with the public, participate in community events, and build relationships with residents to better understand local concerns.

Problem-Solving Approach: Utilizing data-driven methods to identify and address the root causes of crime within specific communities.

Accountability: Implementing mechanisms for community oversight and feedback to ensure police accountability and transparency.

Strengthening Law Enforcement

Strengthening law enforcement capabilities is vital to effectively combat crime and maintain public safety:

Training and Professional Development: Investing in continuous training and professional development for law enforcement personnel to improve investigative skills, crisis response, and de-escalation techniques.

Intelligence and Technology: Enhancing intelligence gathering and sharing among law enforcement agencies, utilizing technology for data analysis and crime mapping to identify hotspots and patterns.

Interagency Collaboration: Promoting cooperation and information-sharing among different law enforcement agencies at the local, state, and federal levels to coordinate efforts and target criminal networks.

Crime Prevention and Social Programs

Crime prevention initiatives and social programs are crucial in addressing the root causes of criminal behavior:

Youth Programs: Investing in education, mentorship, and extracurricular activities to steer youth away from crime and gang involvement.

Job Opportunities: Creating employment opportunities and vocational training programs to reduce economic disparities and provide alternatives to criminal activities.

Substance Abuse Treatment: Expanding access to substance abuse treatment and rehabilitation to address drug-related crime.

Victim Support Services

Providing comprehensive support services for crime victims is essential for their recovery and empowerment:

Crisis Intervention: Immediate assistance, counseling, and trauma support for victims of violent crimes.

Legal Assistance: Ensuring victims have access to legal advice and support throughout the judicial process.

Resource Referrals: Connecting victims with relevant support services, such as shelters, medical care, and financial assistance.

Addressing Corruption and Impunity

Fighting corruption and impunity within law enforcement and judicial institutions is critical for upholding the rule of law:

Strengthening Oversight Mechanisms: Establishing independent oversight bodies to investigate and address allegations of corruption within law enforcement agencies.

Judicial Reforms: Implementing judicial reforms to expedite trials, reduce case backlog, and increase the likelihood of convictions.

Whistleblower Protection: Ensuring robust protection for whistleblowers who expose corrupt practices.

Improving public safety in Mexico demands a comprehensive approach that addresses the root causes of crime, enhances law enforcement capabilities, engages communities, and fosters accountability. By implementing these strategies, Mexico can create a safer and more secure environment, restore public trust in institutions, and work towards a future marked by reduced crime and improved public safety. The commitment of political leaders, law enforcement, civil society, and citizens at large is essential in achieving meaningful progress and ensuring a more peaceful and prosperous Mexico in "The New Power" era of 2024.

HOW CAN INTERNATIONAL COOPERATION HELP COMBAT CRIME IN MEXICO?

International cooperation can play a crucial role in combatting crime in Mexico, especially when dealing with issues that extend beyond national borders. The interconnectedness of crime, particularly drug trafficking and transnational organized crime, requires collaboration among countries to address shared challenges effectively. Here are some ways in which international cooperation can help combat crime in Mexico:

Information Sharing and Intelligence Exchange: Countries can collaborate by sharing information and intelligence on criminal activities, drug trafficking routes, and money laundering networks. This exchange of vital data enhances the ability of law enforcement agencies to track and apprehend criminals operating across borders.

Joint Investigations and Task Forces: Establishing joint investigation teams and international task forces allows law enforcement agencies from different countries to pool resources and expertise in tackling transnational criminal networks. This approach facilitates cross-border operations and arrests, making it harder for criminals to find safe havens in other jurisdictions.

Extradition and Mutual Legal Assistance: Cooperation in the extradition of wanted criminals and the provision of mutual legal assistance enables countries to assist each other in gathering evidence, conducting investigations, and prosecuting offenders involved in cross-border crimes.

Interpol and International Databases: Participation in international law enforcement organizations like Interpol provides access to global databases and tools that aid in identifying and apprehending criminals, locating missing persons, and recovering stolen property.

Border Security and Cooperation: Strengthening border security and collaborating with neighboring countries can help prevent the illegal flow of drugs, weapons, and human trafficking, disrupting the operations of criminal networks.

Cybercrime Collaboration: Given the borderless nature of cybercrime, international cooperation is essential in investigating and prosecuting cybercriminals and sharing best practices for cybersecurity.

Countering Money Laundering: Collaboration in combating money laundering is crucial to disrupt the financial networks of criminal organizations and track illicit financial flows.

Intelligence-Led Operations: Sharing intelligence and expertise with international partners enables better coordination of intelligence-led operations against transnational crime.

Capacity Building and Training: International cooperation can support capacity building and training programs for law enforcement agencies, enhancing their skills in investigating and countering various types of crime.

Addressing Drug Demand: International cooperation can also focus on addressing the demand for illicit drugs in consumer countries, as reducing drug consumption can impact the profitability of drug trafficking.

International cooperation is essential for Mexico to combat crime effectively, particularly when dealing with transnational criminal networks. By collaborating with other countries, sharing information, and pooling resources, Mexico can strengthen its efforts to dismantle criminal organizations, disrupt illegal activities, and enhance public safety. A united front against crime ensures that criminals have no safe haven and increases the likelihood of successfully apprehending and prosecuting offenders involved in cross-border criminal activities. In "The New Power" era of 2024, fostering international cooperation will be instrumental in achieving a safer and more secure Mexico.

HOW CAN MEXICO ADDRESS DRUG DEMAND?

Addressing drug demand in Mexico requires a multifaceted approach that involves preventive measures, public health initiatives, and social interventions. By focusing on reducing drug consumption and addiction, Mexico can undermine the profitability of drug trafficking and break the cycle of drug-related crime. Here are some strategies to address drug demand effectively:

Public Awareness and Education: Implement comprehensive drug education programs in schools and communities to raise awareness about the risks and consequences of drug use. Promote evidence-based information to debunk myths surrounding drugs and encourage informed decision-making.

Treatment and Rehabilitation: Expand access to drug treatment and rehabilitation services for individuals struggling with drug addiction. Provide a range of treatment options, including counseling, therapy, and medication-assisted treatment, to address the specific needs of different individuals.

Decriminalization of Drug Use: Consider decriminalizing drug use and possession for personal use, focusing on public health interventions rather than punitive measures. Redirect resources towards treatment and support programs for drug users instead of arresting and imprisoning them.

Harm Reduction Programs: Establish harm reduction programs that provide clean needles, supervised injection facilities, and naloxone distribution to prevent drug overdose deaths and reduce the spread of infectious diseases.

Community Support and Engagement: Foster a supportive community environment that encourages individuals to seek help for drug-related issues without fear of stigma or discrimination. Involve community leaders and organizations in raising awareness and promoting healthy lifestyles.

Alternatives to Incarceration: Explore alternatives to incarceration for non-violent drug offenders, such as diversion programs or drug courts that focus on treatment and rehabilitation instead of punishment.

Early Intervention: Implement early intervention programs that identify at-risk individuals, such as adolescents experimenting with drugs, and provide support and guidance to prevent drug use from escalating.

Targeted Messaging: Tailor prevention messages to different demographics and populations, considering cultural, social, and economic factors that influence drug use.

Collaboration with Healthcare Providers: Work closely with healthcare providers to identify and address substance use disorders early on. Encourage screening and brief interventions in medical settings.

International Collaboration: Collaborate with other countries to address drug demand on a global scale. Share best practices and learn from successful drug demand reduction initiatives in other countries.

Addressing drug demand is a crucial component of Mexico's efforts to combat drug trafficking and related crime. By adopting preventive measures, expanding treatment and rehabilitation services, and promoting harm reduction and early intervention programs, Mexico can reduce drug consumption and addiction, leading to a safer and healthier society. Collaboration with international partners and a sustained commitment to evidence-based approaches will be essential in achieving success in reducing drug demand and breaking the grip of drug-related problems in "The New Power" era of 2024.

ECONOMIC POLICIES AND SOCIAL WELFARE

In the pursuit of "The New Power" in 2024, economic policies and social welfare play a central role in shaping Mexico's political landscape and ensuring the well-being of its citizens. Balancing economic growth with social equity becomes paramount to address socio-economic disparities, reduce poverty, and foster a more inclusive and prosperous society. This chapter explores the importance of economic policies and social welfare initiatives in Mexico, examining the challenges faced and the strategies required to achieve sustainable development and uplift the lives of all citizens.

Economic Policies for Sustainable Development

Mexico's economic policies should be geared towards achieving sustainable development and fostering economic growth that benefits all segments of society:

Investment in Infrastructure: Infrastructure development, such as transportation, energy, and communication, boosts productivity, creates jobs, and facilitates regional development.

Diversification of Industries: Promote the diversification of industries to reduce reliance on a single sector, making the economy more resilient to external shocks.

Entrepreneurship and Small Businesses: Support entrepreneurship and small businesses through access to finance, training, and technical assistance, fostering innovation and job creation.

Trade and Foreign Investment: Encourage international trade and attract foreign direct investment to stimulate economic growth and create employment opportunities.

Inclusive Economic Growth: Ensure economic growth benefits all citizens by implementing policies that address income inequality and prioritize poverty reduction.

Social Welfare Initiatives for Inclusive Society

Social welfare initiatives are vital to protect vulnerable populations and ensure social inclusion:

Poverty Alleviation Programs: Implement targeted social programs, such as conditional cash transfers and food assistance, to uplift those living in poverty and reduce income disparities.

Universal Healthcare Coverage: Strengthen the healthcare system to ensure universal access to quality healthcare services, improving public health outcomes.

Education and Skill Development: Enhance access to quality education and skill development programs to equip citizens with the tools to participate in the workforce and contribute to economic growth.

Affordable Housing: Address housing affordability challenges through affordable housing programs and support for low-income families.

Social Safety Nets: Establish robust social safety nets to provide support during economic downturns and emergencies, ensuring basic needs are met.

Challenges and Strategies

Challenges in implementing economic policies and social welfare initiatives include:

Fiscal Constraints: Striking a balance between social spending and fiscal responsibility requires prudent financial management.

Corruption and Inefficiency: Combat corruption and enhance administrative efficiency to ensure resources reach the intended beneficiaries.

Regional Disparities: Address regional disparities in economic development and social welfare access through targeted regional development policies.

Collaboration with Private Sector: Collaborate with the private sector to create inclusive business models that promote social responsibility and community development.

Economic policies and social welfare initiatives are integral to Mexico's journey towards "The New Power" era in 2024. By implementing sustainable economic policies, fostering inclusive growth, and prioritizing social welfare programs, Mexico can create a more equitable and prosperous society. Collaboration between government, private sector, civil society, and international partners will be essential in achieving tangible progress and ensuring that economic development benefits all citizens, particularly the most vulnerable. In "The New Power" era, Mexico can aspire to become a model of balanced and sustainable development, driving positive change and uplifting the lives of its people.

ECONOMIC CHALLENGES AND OPPORTUNITIES FOR MEXICO

As Mexico embarks on "The New Power" era in 2024, the country faces a range of economic challenges and opportunities that will shape its political and social landscape. Addressing these challenges and seizing opportunities becomes crucial in fostering sustainable economic growth, reducing inequalities, and improving the well-being of its citizens. This chapter delves into the economic challenges Mexico faces, explores the potential opportunities, and outlines strategies to navigate these waters and unlock Mexico's full economic potential.

Economic Challenges

Income Inequality: Mexico grapples with significant income disparities, with a substantial portion of the population living in poverty. Addressing income inequality is essential for creating a more inclusive economy.

Informal Economy: A large informal economy hinders tax collection, reduces labor protections, and limits access to social benefits for workers.

Dependence on Oil: Mexico's economy has historically relied heavily on oil revenues, making it vulnerable to fluctuations in global oil prices.

Regional Disparities: Regional imbalances in economic development persist, with some states lagging behind in terms of infrastructure and economic opportunities.

Corruption and Transparency: Corruption within the public sector undermines investor confidence, hampers economic growth, and deters foreign investment.

Education and Skills Gap: The education system faces challenges in providing relevant and high-quality education, leading to a skills gap in the labor market.

Economic Opportunities

Manufacturing and Exporting: Mexico's strategic location and trade agreements offer opportunities for growth in the manufacturing and exporting sectors.

Renewable Energy: Investing in renewable energy sources can reduce dependence on oil, promote sustainability, and create new job opportunities.

Innovation and Technology: Fostering innovation and adopting technology can drive productivity and competitiveness across industries.

Tourism: Mexico's rich culture, diverse landscapes, and historical sites offer immense potential for further developing its tourism industry.

Human Capital: Investing in education and skills development can enhance human capital, providing a competitive edge in the global economy.

Strategies for Economic Progress

Inclusive Growth: Implement policies that promote inclusive economic growth, focusing on reducing income inequality and improving opportunities for all.

Diversification: Encourage diversification of the economy to reduce dependence on oil and increase resilience to external shocks.

Infrastructure Investment: Invest in infrastructure development to improve connectivity, support regional development, and attract investments.

Corruption and Governance Reforms: Implement robust governance and anti-corruption reforms to enhance transparency, accountability, and investor confidence.

Human Capital Development: Strengthen the education system and invest in skills development to equip the workforce with the necessary tools for the future.

Public-Private Partnerships: Foster collaboration between the public and private sectors to drive investment, innovation, and economic development.

Navigating economic challenges and seizing opportunities is critical for Mexico's progress in "The New Power" era of 2024. By addressing income inequality, reducing dependence on oil, promoting innovation, and enhancing governance, Mexico can position itself as a dynamic and prosperous nation. A commitment to inclusive growth, sustainable development, and strategic reforms will be instrumental in unlocking Mexico's full economic potential and creating a brighter future for all its citizens.

SOCIAL WELFARE PROGRAMS AND POVERTY ALLEVIATION

In the pursuit of "The New Power" in Mexico, social welfare programs and poverty alleviation are critical pillars to uplift the lives of the most vulnerable citizens, reduce socio-economic disparities, and promote inclusive growth. As Mexico approaches the year 2024, this chapter explores the importance of social welfare initiatives, the challenges faced in poverty alleviation, and the strategies required to strengthen social safety nets and create a more equitable and prosperous society for all.

The Importance of Social Welfare Programs

Social welfare programs play a vital role in providing essential support to those facing economic hardship and addressing social inequalities:

1. Poverty Reduction: Social welfare programs target poverty at its roots by providing financial assistance and support to families living below the poverty line.

2. Access to Basic Needs: These programs ensure access to basic needs such as food, healthcare, and housing, enhancing the overall well-being of vulnerable populations.

3. Education and Skill Development: Investing in education and skill development programs empowers individuals to break the cycle of poverty and secure better opportunities for the future.

4. Social Safety Nets: Social welfare initiatives create safety nets for individuals and families during times of economic uncertainty, reducing the impact of financial shocks.

Challenges in Poverty Alleviation

While social welfare programs are essential, various challenges must be addressed to achieve effective poverty alleviation:

1. Targeting the Most Vulnerable: Ensuring that social welfare programs reach the most vulnerable populations and those most in need is critical for their success.

2. Fiscal Constraints: Allocating sufficient financial resources to social welfare programs can be challenging, given other budgetary priorities.

3. Administrative Efficiency: Streamlining administrative processes and reducing bureaucratic barriers can improve the efficiency and effectiveness of these programs.

4. Sustainable Impact: Ensuring that social welfare initiatives have a lasting impact by addressing root causes of poverty and empowering individuals to become self-sufficient.

Strategies for Effective Poverty Alleviation

To strengthen social welfare programs and achieve meaningful poverty alleviation, Mexico can consider the following strategies:

Targeted Approach: Identify and target the most vulnerable populations, such as low-income families, single-parent households, and the elderly, to ensure resources are directed where they are needed most.

Data-Driven Policies: Utilize data and evidence-based approaches to design and implement social welfare programs, ensuring that interventions are effective and tailored to specific needs.

Comprehensive Support: Create comprehensive support systems that address multiple dimensions of poverty, including access to education, healthcare, housing, and employment opportunities.

Public-Private Partnerships: Foster collaborations with private sector entities to support skill development, job training, and employment opportunities for marginalized communities.

Evaluation and Monitoring: Regularly evaluate the impact of social welfare programs to identify areas of improvement and ensure that resources are allocated effectively.

Social welfare programs and poverty alleviation are integral components of "The New Power" era in Mexico. By strengthening social safety nets, targeting the most vulnerable, and implementing data-driven policies, Mexico can make significant strides in reducing poverty and creating a more inclusive society. The commitment of political leaders, collaboration with civil society organizations, and sustainable allocation of resources will be essential in achieving lasting poverty alleviation and promoting the well-being and dignity of all Mexican citizens. In "The New Power" era of 2024, Mexico can emerge as a nation that prioritizes social welfare and demonstrates its dedication to uplifting the lives of its most marginalized populations.

EDUCATION AND YOUTH EMPOWERMENT

In "The New Power" era of 2024, the role of education and youth empowerment becomes paramount in shaping Mexico's political landscape and driving socio-economic progress. Investing in education and empowering the youth are key strategies to foster a skilled, innovative, and engaged citizenry that can contribute to the nation's development. This chapter explores the importance of education, the challenges faced, and the strategies required to empower Mexican youth and create a brighter future for the country.

The Importance of Education

Education serves as a cornerstone for societal progress and individual empowerment:

1. Human Capital Development: Education equips individuals with knowledge, skills, and capabilities that drive economic growth and development.

2. Empowering the Youth: Investing in the youth empowers them to be active participants in shaping their future and contributing to the nation's growth.

3. Social Mobility: Quality education enables social mobility, allowing individuals from disadvantaged backgrounds to overcome barriers and access better opportunities.

4. Innovation and Progress: A well-educated population fosters innovation, creativity, and critical thinking, driving advancements in various fields.

Challenges in Education and Youth Empowerment

Despite the importance of education and youth empowerment, several challenges hinder progress:

1. Education Quality: Ensuring quality education that is relevant and equips students with essential skills remains a challenge.

2. Access to Education: Some communities, particularly in remote and marginalized areas, lack access to quality education.

3. Dropout Rates: High dropout rates in schools hinder educational attainment and future opportunities for youth.

4. Skills Gap: There is a mismatch between the skills provided by the education system and the needs of the job market.

Strategies for Youth Empowerment

To empower Mexican youth and foster a thriving future, several strategies can be implemented:

1. Enhancing Education Quality: Improve the quality of education by updating curricula, promoting active learning, and providing professional development for teachers.

2. Access to Education: Invest in infrastructure and resources to ensure all children, regardless of their location, have access to quality education.

3. Vocational and Technical Training: Expand vocational and technical training opportunities to bridge the skills gap and meet the demands of the job market.

4. Youth Entrepreneurship: Support youth entrepreneurship initiatives and start-up programs to foster innovation and job creation.

5. Mentorship and Career Guidance: Provide mentorship and career guidance programs to help youth explore diverse career paths and make informed decisions.

6. Digital Literacy: Enhance digital literacy skills to prepare youth for the digital economy and the challenges of the Fourth Industrial Revolution.

Education and youth empowerment are essential pillars of "The New Power" era in Mexico. By prioritizing education quality, expanding access to education, and fostering youth entrepreneurship and innovation, Mexico can create a skilled and engaged workforce ready to face the challenges of the future. A commitment to investing in education and empowering the youth will not only contribute to socio-economic progress but also strengthen Mexico's democratic fabric and ensure a brighter and more prosperous future for all its citizens. In "The New Power" era of 2024, Mexico can emerge as a nation that values its youth as catalysts for positive change and development.

REFORMS IN THE EDUCATION SYSTEM

In "The New Power" era of 2024, reforming the education system in Mexico becomes a vital aspect of transforming the country's political landscape and ensuring a brighter future for its citizens. A robust and inclusive education system is the bedrock of progress, empowering individuals, fostering innovation, and driving socio-economic development. This chapter explores the importance of education reforms, the challenges faced in the process, and the strategies required to revitalize the education system and propel Mexico towards a more prosperous and equitable society.

The Importance of Education Reforms

Education reforms are essential for the following reasons:

Quality Education: Reforms aim to improve the quality of education, ensuring that students receive relevant and up-to-date knowledge and skills.

Equal Opportunities: Reforms work towards providing equal educational opportunities to all, regardless of socio-economic backgrounds or geographical locations.

Global Competitiveness: A reformed education system equips students to compete on a global scale and participate in the knowledge-based economy.

Modernization: Reforms incorporate innovative teaching methods, technology integration, and digital literacy to prepare students for the future job market.

Challenges in Implementing Education Reforms

Implementing education reforms can be met with various challenges:

Resistance to Change: Resistance from stakeholders, including teachers' unions and traditional educational institutions, can hinder reform efforts.

Funding Constraints: Adequate funding is required to implement and sustain educational reforms effectively.

Teacher Training: Proper training and professional development for teachers are crucial to ensure they are equipped to deliver the reformed curriculum effectively.

Balancing Local and National Needs: Striking a balance between national educational standards and regional or cultural variations can be challenging.

Strategies for Effective Education Reforms

To achieve successful education reforms, the following strategies can be employed:

Inclusive Stakeholder Engagement: Involve all stakeholders, including teachers, parents, students, and policymakers, in the reform process to ensure ownership and support.

Adequate Funding: Allocate sufficient resources and funding to support the implementation of reforms, including teacher training and infrastructure development.

Professional Development for Teachers: Invest in continuous professional development for teachers to enhance their pedagogical skills and subject knowledge.

Technology Integration: Embrace technology in education, providing access to digital resources and tools to enhance learning experiences.

Curriculum Review: Regularly review and update the curriculum to align with the changing needs of the job market and society.

Data-Driven Approaches: Use data to monitor the progress and impact of reforms, making evidence-based decisions for further improvements.

Education reforms are essential to shaping "The New Power" era in Mexico. By prioritizing quality education, inclusive stakeholder engagement, and adequate funding, Mexico can establish an education system that empowers its citizens and prepares them for the challenges and opportunities of the future. Despite the challenges, a commitment to educational transformation is an investment in Mexico's long-term prosperity and development. In "The New Power" era of 2024, Mexico can take bold strides towards building an education system that nurtures talent, fosters innovation, and fosters a well-informed, skilled, and engaged citizenry ready to lead the nation towards a brighter and more prosperous future.

EMPOWERING YOUTH FOR A STRONGER FUTURE

In "The New Power" era of 2024, empowering the youth becomes a pivotal strategy to shape Mexico's political landscape and drive social and economic progress. As the country's most valuable asset, the youth hold the key to Mexico's future prosperity and success. This chapter explores the significance of empowering the youth, the challenges faced in the process, and the strategies required to harness their potential and build a stronger and more dynamic future for Mexico.

The Significance of Youth Empowerment

Empowering the youth is essential for the following reasons:

Agents of Change: Youth are catalysts for positive change, driving innovation, and challenging the status quo.

Shaping Political Discourse: Engaging the youth in politics empowers them to shape policy agendas and advocate for issues that matter to them.

Economic Growth: Empowered youth contribute to the workforce, entrepreneurship, and economic growth, unlocking Mexico's full potential.

Social Inclusivity: Youth empowerment promotes inclusivity, ensuring that all segments of society have a voice and opportunities for advancement.

Challenges in Youth Empowerment

While youth empowerment is crucial, several challenges must be addressed:

Access to Quality Education: Ensuring all youth have access to quality education that prepares them for the job market and fosters critical thinking.

Youth Unemployment: Addressing youth unemployment and underemployment by creating job opportunities and supporting entrepreneurship.

Political Participation: Encouraging youth engagement in politics and governance, overcoming apathy and disenchantment.

Youth Representation: Advocating for increased youth representation in decision-making bodies and political institutions.

Strategies for Youth Empowerment

To empower the youth and create a stronger future, the following strategies can be employed:

Quality Education: Ensure access to quality education that fosters critical thinking, creativity, and relevant skills for the job market.

Job Creation and Entrepreneurship: Promote job creation, particularly in emerging sectors, and support youth entrepreneurship through training and funding opportunities.

Youth Inclusion in Governance: Create platforms for youth to participate in political processes, allowing them to influence policy decisions.

Mentorship and Skill Development: Establish mentorship programs that connect youth with experienced professionals and provide skill development opportunities.

Digital Literacy: Foster digital literacy to equip youth with the necessary digital skills for the modern world.

Advocacy for Youth Rights: Advocate for the rights of youth, including access to healthcare, education, and opportunities for civic engagement.

Empowering the youth is a pivotal pillar of "The New Power" era in Mexico. By investing in quality education, job creation, and youth inclusion in governance, Mexico can harness the energy and creativity of its youth to drive socio-economic progress and political transformation. Addressing the challenges faced by young people and providing them with opportunities and support are investments in Mexico's future prosperity and stability. In "The New Power" era of 2024, Mexico has the opportunity to embrace its youth as agents of change and empower them to build a stronger, more inclusive, and dynamic nation.

POLITICAL PARTICIPATION AND ELECTIONS

POLITICAL PARTIES AND ELECTORAL DYNAMICS

In "The New Power" era of 2024, political parties and electoral dynamics play a crucial role in shaping Mexico's political landscape. As the nation navigates the challenges and opportunities of the future, understanding the intricacies of the political party system and electoral processes is essential for effective governance and citizen participation. This chapter explores the significance of political parties, the dynamics of elections, and the impact they have on Mexico's political trajectory.

The Role of Political Parties

Political parties serve as key actors in Mexico's democratic process and governance:

Representation: Political parties represent diverse ideologies, interests, and constituencies, giving voice to different segments of society.

Policy Formulation: Parties develop policy agendas and platforms that shape the national and regional policy landscape.

Candidate Selection: Political parties nominate candidates for elected offices, offering citizens choices in leadership.

Electoral Competition: Parties engage in electoral competition, vying for votes and control of government institutions.

Electoral Dynamics

Understanding electoral dynamics is vital in comprehending Mexico's political scene:

Voter Turnout: Analyzing voter turnout trends sheds light on citizen engagement and political participation.

Electoral Alliances: Examining electoral alliances illuminates how parties collaborate to strengthen their electoral prospects.

Incumbency Advantage: Understanding the incumbency advantage helps grasp the challenges faced by opposition parties.

Voter Demographics: Analyzing voter demographics provides insights into voting patterns and party support.

Challenges in Electoral Dynamics

Several challenges impact electoral dynamics in Mexico:

Voter Apathy: Voter apathy can hinder political participation and weaken democratic legitimacy.

Electoral Violence: Electoral violence poses a threat to free and fair elections and undermines democratic values.

Political Corruption: The influence of political corruption on electoral processes erodes public trust in the political system.

Media Influence: Media biases and misinformation can sway voter opinions and affect electoral outcomes.

Strategies for Strengthening Electoral Dynamics

To enhance electoral dynamics, the following strategies can be employed:

Voter Education: Promote voter education to increase civic awareness and engagement.

Electoral Reforms: Implement reforms to address electoral violence, campaign financing, and party registration.

Transparency and Accountability: Foster transparency and accountability to combat political corruption and promote fair elections.

Media Literacy: Promote media literacy to empower voters to critically evaluate information.

In "The New Power" era of 2024, understanding the role of political parties and electoral dynamics is crucial for Mexico's political development and governance. By strengthening democratic institutions, encouraging voter participation, and addressing electoral challenges, Mexico can build a more resilient and responsive political system. A commitment to free and fair elections, open political discourse, and citizen engagement will be instrumental in shaping Mexico's political trajectory and fostering a nation that is politically dynamic, inclusive, and responsive to the needs of its citizens. In "The New Power" era, Mexico can rise as a model of democratic excellence, inspiring positive change and progress for years to come.

OVERVIEW OF MAJOR POLITICAL PARTIES IN MEXICO

In "The New Power" era of 2024, the political landscape of Mexico is shaped by several major political parties, each with its own ideologies, agendas, and historical significance. Understanding these parties is essential for comprehending Mexico's political dynamics and the diverse choices available to voters. This chapter provides an overview of the major political parties in Mexico, delving into their histories, key principles, and roles in shaping the nation's governance and policies.

National Action Party (PAN)

History: Founded in 1939, the PAN initially emerged as a conservative and Catholic-oriented party. Over time, it transformed into a center-right party promoting free market policies and individual liberties.

Key Principles: The PAN advocates for limited government intervention, fiscal responsibility, and social conservatism. It emphasizes family values and has historically been associated with Mexico's business elites.

Role: The PAN has been a major player in Mexican politics, holding the presidency for two terms (2000-2012) with Vicente Fox and Felipe Calderón. It has also controlled several states and municipalities.

Institutional Revolutionary Party (PRI)

History: The PRI is one of the oldest and historically most dominant parties in Mexico. Established in 1929, it dominated Mexican politics for over seven decades.

Key Principles: Initially a center-left party with socialist leanings, the PRI shifted to a centrist ideology, promoting state-led development and social programs.

Role: For much of its history, the PRI held a one-party rule and maintained political hegemony through a clientelist system. In recent years, it faced challenges from opposition parties but remains influential.

Party of the Democratic Revolution (PRD)

History: Formed in 1989, the PRD emerged from a split in the PRI and was initially a leftist party that advocated for social justice and progressive policies.

Key Principles: The PRD is known for its advocacy of workers' rights, social welfare programs, and democratic reforms. It aims to counteract the influence of the business elites.

Role: The PRD has been a significant opposition party and has had periods of influence at the local and state levels.

Morena (National Regeneration Movement)

History: Established in 2014, Morena is a relatively new party founded by Andrés Manuel López Obrador (AMLO), who became the President of Mexico in 2018.

Key Principles: Morena embraces progressive and left-wing principles, focusing on anti-corruption, social justice, and empowering marginalized communities.

Role: Morena's rapid rise to power led to its presidential victory and control of both houses of Congress in 2018. It aims to lead Mexico's transformation under AMLO's leadership.

In "The New Power" era of 2024, Mexico's political landscape is characterized by a diverse range of major political parties. Each party brings its unique history, ideologies, and role in shaping the nation's political discourse and governance. Understanding the major political parties provides voters with the opportunity to make informed decisions and actively participate in shaping Mexico's future. The interplay between these parties will determine the course of Mexico's political trajectory and its ability to address the challenges and seize the opportunities of the future. In "The New Power" era, Mexico's political parties play a pivotal role in determining the nation's destiny, making it imperative to stay informed and engaged in the democratic process.

ANALYSIS OF ELECTORAL TRENDS

In "The New Power" era of 2024, analyzing electoral trends is crucial for understanding the evolving political dynamics in Mexico. Examining past electoral patterns and emerging trends provides valuable insights into voter behavior, party performance, and the changing preferences of the electorate. This chapter delves into the analysis of electoral trends in Mexico, exploring the factors that have influenced election outcomes and the implications for the country's political landscape.

Shift in Voter Demographics

Analyzing changes in voter demographics sheds light on shifting political allegiances:

Youth Vote: The increasing influence of the youth vote, driven by issues such as education, employment, and social justice, can sway election outcomes.

Urban-Rural Divide: The disparity between urban and rural areas in terms of access to resources and opportunities influences voting patterns.

Gender Dynamics: The growing importance of women voters and gender-related policies in elections has significant implications for political parties.

Rise of Anti-Incumbency Sentiment

Voters' dissatisfaction with incumbent governments has led to an increase in anti-incumbency sentiment:

Corruption and Governance: Public frustration with corruption and ineffective governance has fueled support for opposition parties.

Economic Performance: Voters' perception of the government's handling of the economy can significantly impact electoral outcomes.

Security Concerns: Addressing issues of crime and security is a top priority for voters, and parties' responses to these concerns can influence election results.

Impact of Social Media and Digital Platforms

The role of social media and digital platforms in shaping political discourse and mobilizing voters cannot be overlooked:

Influence on Public Opinion: Social media has become a powerful tool in shaping public opinion and driving political narratives.

Online Campaigning: Parties' effectiveness in utilizing digital platforms for campaigning can influence voter engagement and turnout.

Disinformation and Misinformation: The spread of disinformation and misinformation on social media can impact voter perceptions and decisions.

Electoral Alliances and Coalition Building

Parties' strategies for forming electoral alliances can have a significant impact on election outcomes:

Strength in Unity: Parties forming alliances can pool their resources and broaden their appeal to the electorate.

Ideological Compatibility: Aligning with like-minded parties can reinforce a common agenda and attract a broader voter base.

Regional Impact: Electoral alliances can have a varying impact on different regions, leading to localized outcomes.

In "The New Power" era of 2024, understanding electoral trends is vital for anticipating Mexico's political trajectory and governance. The analysis of voter demographics, anti-incumbency sentiment, the role of social media, and electoral alliances provides valuable insights for political parties, policymakers, and citizens. By staying attuned to electoral trends, Mexico can navigate the changing political landscape more effectively and strengthen its democratic processes. The decisions made by parties and voters in response to these trends will shape the nation's political future and determine its ability to address challenges and embrace opportunities. In "The New Power" era, being cognizant of electoral trends empowers Mexico to move forward with informed choices and democratic excellence.

ELECTORAL PROCESSES AND VOTER ENGAGEMENT

In "The New Power" era of 2024, electoral processes and voter engagement are central to the strength and vibrancy of Mexico's democracy. A well-functioning electoral system and active citizen participation are essential for ensuring fair representation and a government that reflects the will of the people. This chapter explores the electoral processes in Mexico, the challenges faced in fostering voter engagement, and the strategies required to promote a more engaged and participatory electorate.

Electoral Processes in Mexico

Voter Registration: Understanding the voter registration process and ensuring an inclusive and updated voter list is vital for a fair and transparent electoral system.

Electoral Commissions: The role of electoral commissions, such as the National Electoral Institute (INE), in organizing elections, ensuring their integrity, and resolving disputes.

Election Campaigns: Analyzing the rules and regulations governing election campaigns, campaign financing, and media access for political parties.

Election Day Procedures: Examining the voting process, ballot security, and mechanisms for ensuring the integrity of the election results.

Challenges in Voter Engagement

Voter Apathy: Addressing voter apathy and disengagement, particularly among young and marginalized populations.

Disinformation and Misinformation: Tackling the spread of false information that can influence voter decisions.

Inclusivity: Ensuring that all eligible voters, including those in remote and marginalized areas, have access to the polls.

Voter Education: Promoting voter education to increase civic awareness and understanding of the electoral process.

Strategies for Promoting Voter Engagement

Voter Education Campaigns: Launching voter education campaigns to inform citizens about their voting rights, the electoral process, and the importance of their participation.

Enhancing Digital Engagement: Leveraging digital platforms and social media to reach and engage with a broader audience.

Civic Education in Schools: Incorporating civic education into school curricula to instill a sense of civic responsibility and active citizenship from an early age.

Encouraging Youth Participation: Creating youth-friendly initiatives and platforms to encourage young people's participation in the electoral process.

Voter Outreach Programs: Implementing voter outreach programs to reach marginalized communities and ensure their voices are heard.

In "The New Power" era of 2024, electoral processes and voter engagement are critical pillars of Mexico's democratic progress. By fostering transparent and inclusive electoral processes, addressing voter apathy, and promoting voter education and digital engagement, Mexico can create a more engaged and participatory electorate. A commitment to citizen participation and active civic engagement will strengthen Mexico's democratic foundation and ensure that the government is truly representative of the people's will. In "The New Power" era, Mexico has the opportunity to revitalize its electoral processes and empower citizens to be active participants in shaping the nation's future.

UNDERSTANDING MEXICAN ELECTIONS AND THEIR SIGNIFICANCE

In "The New Power" era of 2024, Mexican elections hold significant importance in shaping the country's political trajectory and determining the course of its governance. Understanding the electoral process, from campaign dynamics to the impact of election outcomes, is essential for citizens, political actors, and policymakers alike. This chapter explores the significance of Mexican elections, the mechanics of the electoral process, and the implications of electoral outcomes on the nation's political landscape.

The Electoral System in Mexico

The Presidency: Mexico follows a presidential system, where the President is both the head of state and head of government, serving a single six-year term without the possibility of re-election.

Congress: The Mexican Congress consists of two chambers - the Senate (with 128 seats) and the Chamber of Deputies (with 500 seats). Members of both chambers are elected through a mixed-member proportional representation system.

Local Elections: In addition to federal elections, Mexico holds regular local elections to elect state governors, mayors, and local representatives.

Campaigning and Political Parties

Political Parties: An overview of major political parties and their ideologies, as well as their roles in election campaigns and governance.

Campaign Finance: The rules and regulations governing campaign financing and the impact of money in politics.

Campaign Strategies: The tactics employed by political parties and candidates to mobilize support and win votes.

Voter Participation and Turnout

Voter Turnout Trends: Analyzing historical voter turnout patterns and the factors influencing voter participation.

Voter Demographics: Understanding how age, gender, and regional factors impact voter turnout.

Election Monitoring and Transparency

Electoral Observers: The role of domestic and international election observers in ensuring free and fair elections.

Transparency and Accountability: The importance of transparency in the electoral process to maintain public trust.

Implications of Electoral Outcomes

Government Formation: The process of forming a government after an election and the potential for coalition governments.

Policy Priorities: How electoral outcomes influence policy agendas and government priorities.

Democratic Legitimacy: The impact of election results on the legitimacy of government and democratic institutions.

In "The New Power" era of 2024, understanding Mexican elections is fundamental for active citizenship and informed decision-making. By grasping the mechanics of the electoral process, recognizing the significance of voter participation, and comprehending the implications of electoral outcomes, citizens can actively engage in shaping the nation's governance. Moreover, transparency and accountability in the electoral system contribute to strengthening Mexico's democratic foundation. In "The New Power" era, Mexico's elections serve as a platform for citizen voices, shaping the nation's future, and fostering a responsive and inclusive political landscape.

FACTORS INFLUENCING VOTER TURNOUT AND BEHAVIOR

In "The New Power" era of 2024, understanding the factors that influence voter turnout and behavior is crucial for fostering an engaged and participatory electorate in Mexico. Voter participation is a cornerstone of democracy, and identifying the drivers and barriers to voter turnout provides valuable insights for political parties, policymakers, and citizens. This chapter explores the key factors that impact voter participation and behavior, shedding light on how they shape Mexico's political landscape.

Socioeconomic Factors

Income and Education: Higher levels of education and income tend to correlate with increased voter participation, as individuals with more resources are more likely to be politically informed and motivated to vote.

Employment Status: The availability of time and flexibility in work schedules can influence a person's ability to vote on Election Day.

Geographic Location: Voters in rural or remote areas may face logistical challenges in accessing polling stations, affecting their voter turnout.

Demographic Factors

Age: Younger voters often have lower turnout rates compared to older age groups, although efforts to engage youth can positively impact their participation.

Gender: Gender dynamics can influence voting behavior, with women and men sometimes showing different preferences and priorities.

Ethnicity and Culture: Cultural factors can play a role in shaping voter behavior, with distinct voting patterns in different ethnic or cultural communities.

Political Context and Campaign Dynamics

Incumbency: Voter behavior may be influenced by the performance and popularity of incumbents, leading to anti-incumbency sentiment or support for continuity.

Campaign Appeals: The messaging, promises, and strategies of political campaigns can sway voter preferences and mobilize support.

Media and Social Media: The influence of media and social media on shaping voter perceptions and political discourse.

Electoral Rules and Accessibility

Voter Registration: An efficient and accessible voter registration process is essential for ensuring citizens' inclusion in the electoral process.

Polling Station Locations: The proximity and accessibility of polling stations can impact voter turnout, particularly in remote or marginalized areas.

Voting Methods: The ease of voting methods, such as in-person voting, mail-in voting, or electronic voting, can influence participation rates.

Civic Engagement and Social Norms

Civic Education: Education on civics and the importance of political participation can encourage citizens to become more politically engaged.

Social Norms and Peer Influence: Social pressures and influence from friends, family, or community members can impact voter behavior.

In "The New Power" era of 2024, recognizing the factors that influence voter turnout and behavior empowers Mexico to strengthen its democratic foundation. By addressing socioeconomic disparities, engaging youth and marginalized communities, and promoting civic education, Mexico can enhance voter participation and create a more inclusive and representative political landscape. Moreover, understanding the dynamics of political campaigns, media influence, and electoral accessibility contributes to fostering an informed and engaged electorate. In "The New Power" era, Mexico has the opportunity to harness the potential of its citizens, ensuring that their voices are heard and their choices shape the nation's future.

SHAPING MEXICO'S ROLE ON THE GLOBAL STAGE

FOREIGN POLICY AND DIPLOMACY

In "The New Power" era of 2024, Mexico's foreign policy and diplomacy play a crucial role in shaping the nation's position in the global arena. As the world becomes increasingly interconnected, Mexico faces both challenges and opportunities in navigating international relations. This chapter explores Mexico's approach to foreign policy, the key challenges it encounters, and the opportunities it can seize to further its interests on the global stage.

Mexico's Foreign Policy Principles

Non-Intervention: Mexico upholds the principle of non-intervention, advocating for peaceful resolution of conflicts and respecting the sovereignty of other nations.

Multilateralism: Mexico emphasizes multilateral approaches to global challenges, actively participating in international organizations and forums.

Free Trade and Economic Integration: Mexico seeks to strengthen economic ties and trade relationships through agreements such as the United States-Mexico-Canada Agreement (USMCA) and participation in regional economic blocs.

Promotion of Human Rights: Mexico advocates for human rights and inclusivity in international forums, voicing concerns on issues like migration and refugees.

Challenges in International Relations

Security and Transnational Crime: Addressing transnational crime, drug trafficking, and security issues remain significant challenges for Mexico in its relations with neighboring countries and beyond.

Immigration and Border Relations: Managing immigration flows and maintaining balanced border relations with the United States presents ongoing complexities.

Climate Change and Environmental Issues: As a responsible global citizen, Mexico faces the challenge of addressing climate change and promoting sustainable development.

Economic Diversification: Seeking to diversify trade and investment partners in the face of economic uncertainties and geopolitical shifts.

Opportunities in the Global Arena

Economic Diplomacy: Leveraging economic partnerships to drive growth, attract foreign investment, and promote Mexican goods and services abroad.

Soft Power: Promoting Mexican culture, arts, and traditions as a form of soft power to build bridges and foster international cooperation.

Climate Leadership: Demonstrating leadership in addressing climate change and positioning Mexico as a global player in sustainable development.

Regional Integration: Engaging proactively with Latin American and Caribbean countries to strengthen regional cooperation and foster common development goals.

In "The New Power" era of 2024, Mexico's foreign policy and diplomacy are crucial in shaping the nation's standing in the global arena. By adhering to its principles of non-intervention and multilateralism, Mexico can actively contribute to international cooperation and peace. Addressing challenges in security, immigration, and environmental sustainability will require strategic diplomatic efforts. Additionally, seizing opportunities in economic diplomacy, soft power promotion, and regional integration can enhance Mexico's global influence and contribute to its prosperity and stability. In "The New Power" era, Mexico has the chance to define its role in the world, projecting itself as an engaged and responsible global actor in pursuit of a prosperous and harmonious future.

MEXICO'S APPROACH TO INTERNATIONAL RELATIONS

Mexico's foreign policy is an essential aspect of its political landscape, shaping its interactions with the international community and influencing its position in global affairs. This chapter delves into Mexico's approach to international relations, highlighting its key principles, objectives, and challenges. By understanding Mexico's engagement on the world stage, we can gain insights into how the nation navigates the complexities of the global arena.

Foreign Policy Principles

At the core of Mexico's approach to international relations are a set of fundamental principles that guide its actions on the global stage:

Non-Intervention

Non-intervention is a cornerstone of Mexican foreign policy. Mexico upholds the principle of respecting the sovereignty and internal affairs of other nations, promoting peaceful coexistence, and refraining from interference in the domestic affairs of other states.

Dispute Resolution through Dialogue

Mexico prioritizes diplomatic dialogue and peaceful conflict resolution. It seeks to resolve disputes through negotiation, mediation, and multilateral forums, fostering stability and regional cooperation.

International Law and Human Rights

Mexico is committed to upholding international law, human rights, and the rule of law in its relations with other nations. It actively participates in international human rights mechanisms and advocates for respect for human rights globally.

Multilateralism and Cooperation

As a proponent of multilateralism, Mexico values cooperation and collaboration with regional and international organizations. It actively engages in forums like the United Nations, the Organization of American

States (OAS), and the Community of Latin American and Caribbean States (CELAC) to address shared challenges.

Promotion of Peace and Security

Mexico strives to promote peace and security globally. It supports initiatives aimed at conflict prevention, disarmament, and counterterrorism efforts.

Priorities in International Relations

Mexico's foreign policy focuses on several key priorities that align with its national interests and values:

Trade and Economic Relations

Mexico is a proponent of free trade and has pursued an open and liberal trade policy. The nation actively participates in international trade agreements, including the United States-Mexico-Canada Agreement (USMCA) and trade agreements with various Latin American and Asian countries.

Migration and Border Cooperation

Given its geographical proximity to the United States and Central America, Mexico places significant importance on migration and border cooperation. It works to address issues related to migration flows, human trafficking, and border security while promoting safe and orderly migration.

Environmental and Climate Change Agenda

As a responsible global actor, Mexico is committed to addressing environmental challenges and climate change. It participates in international efforts to combat climate change, protect biodiversity, and promote sustainable development.

Humanitarian Assistance and Global Development

Mexico actively engages in humanitarian assistance and global development initiatives, supporting countries in crisis and contributing to international development efforts.

Challenges and Opportunities

Mexico faces various challenges in its international relations:

Trade Tensions and Economic Uncertainty

Trade tensions and economic uncertainties in the global arena can impact Mexico's economy, given its close ties to international trade partners like the United States.

Transnational Crime and Drug Trafficking

Transnational crime, including drug trafficking and organized crime, poses security challenges for Mexico and requires cooperation with other nations to address effectively.

Regional Integration and Migration

Strengthening regional integration and addressing migration challenges require cooperation with neighboring countries and regional organizations.

Balancing Global Partnerships

Mexico seeks to balance its engagement with various global powers and international organizations to maintain its sovereignty and independence in decision-making.

Mexico's approach to international relations is shaped by its core principles of non-intervention, peaceful resolution of conflicts, and adherence to international law. As it navigates the complexities of the global arena, Mexico strives to promote peace, security, and cooperation while addressing challenges related to trade, migration, and transnational issues. By maintaining a balanced and principled foreign policy, Mexico seeks to build a more prosperous and stable world for its citizens and the international community.

CHALLENGES AND OPPORTUNITIES IN THE GLOBAL ARENA

As Mexico embraces "The New Power 2024" era, its engagement in the global arena presents a myriad of challenges and opportunities. This chapter explores the complexities of Mexico's interactions with the international community, focusing on the key challenges it faces and the potential opportunities it can harness to shape its future on the world stage.

Economic Challenges and Globalization

Challenge: Mexico's economy is deeply integrated into the global market, making it vulnerable to fluctuations in the global economic landscape. Economic challenges, such as trade tensions, protectionist measures, and currency fluctuations, can impact Mexico's export-oriented industries and foreign direct investment.

Opportunity: Embracing innovation, investing in research and development, and diversifying trade partnerships can enable Mexico to navigate economic challenges and harness the benefits of globalization. By promoting entrepreneurship and supporting small and medium-sized enterprises, Mexico can foster economic resilience and competitiveness.

Climate Change and Environmental Sustainability

Challenge: Mexico faces environmental challenges, including climate change, deforestation, and pollution. As a responsible global actor, it must address the consequences of environmental degradation and contribute to international efforts to combat climate change.

Opportunity: Mexico can seize the opportunity to lead in environmental sustainability. By implementing robust environmental policies, promoting renewable energy sources, and engaging in global climate negotiations, Mexico can play a pivotal role in shaping the international climate agenda.

Migration and Border Security

Challenge: Mexico's proximity to the United States and Central America makes it a critical transit country for migrants seeking better opportunities. Managing migration flows and addressing the root causes of migration present significant challenges.

Opportunity: By fostering dialogue and cooperation with neighboring countries, Mexico can work towards comprehensive migration solutions. It can advocate for a humane and orderly migration system while addressing the needs of migrants and protecting their human rights.

Geopolitical Dynamics and Regional Cooperation

Challenge: Mexico must navigate complex geopolitical dynamics and regional tensions. Striking a balance between its relations with various global powers and engaging in regional cooperation is essential to protect its interests and sovereignty.

Opportunity: By actively participating in regional organizations, such as CELAC and the Pacific Alliance, Mexico can contribute to regional stability and cooperation. Building bridges with neighboring countries and strengthening regional integration can create opportunities for shared prosperity.

Security and Transnational Crime

Challenge: Transnational crime, drug trafficking, and organized crime present significant security challenges for Mexico. Addressing these issues requires robust international cooperation and intelligence-sharing.

Opportunity: By collaborating with other nations and international organizations, Mexico can enhance its security capabilities and tackle transnational crime more effectively. It can also promote social and economic development to address the root causes of criminal activities.

Humanitarian Assistance and Global Development

Challenge: As a responsible global actor, Mexico faces the challenge of providing humanitarian assistance to countries in crisis and contributing to global development efforts despite its own domestic priorities.

Opportunity: By leveraging its experience in disaster response and development assistance, Mexico can increase its humanitarian contributions and play a role in shaping international development policies. Partnering with international organizations and fostering south-south cooperation can maximize its impact.

As Mexico embraces "The New Power 2024," it confronts a diverse set of challenges and opportunities in the global arena. By adopting a proactive and principled approach to international relations, Mexico can navigate the challenges and harness the opportunities to shape its destiny on the world stage. As a responsible global actor, Mexico's actions can inspire positive change, foster regional cooperation, and contribute to building a more prosperous and peaceful world for all.

TRADE AND ECONOMIC PARTNERSHIPS

In "The New Power" era of 2024, trade and economic partnerships play a pivotal role in shaping Mexico's economic growth and international standing. As a country strategically located between North and South America, Mexico has emerged as a global player in trade and investment. This chapter explores Mexico's approach to trade, its economic partnerships, and the opportunities and challenges it faces in a dynamic global economy.

Trade Relations and Agreements

United States-Mexico-Canada Agreement (USMCA): Analyzing the significance of the USMCA in fostering trade integration in North America and its impact on the Mexican economy.

Regional Trade Agreements: Assessing Mexico's participation in regional trade blocs such as the Pacific Alliance and its implications for economic growth.

Bilateral Trade Relations: Examining key bilateral trade relationships with countries like China, the European Union, and other Latin American nations.

Diversification of Trade Partnerships

Reducing Dependency: Exploring Mexico's efforts to diversify its trade partnerships to reduce reliance on a few major trading partners.

Strengthening Ties with Emerging Markets: Assessing opportunities for enhanced trade and investment with emerging economies in Asia, Africa, and the Middle East.

Economic Integration in Latin America

Pacific Alliance: Understanding the role of the Pacific Alliance in promoting economic integration and cooperation among its member countries.

ProMéxico: Analyzing the role of ProMéxico in promoting foreign investment and facilitating trade opportunities for Mexican businesses abroad.

Challenges and Opportunities in the Global Economy

Global Supply Chain Disruptions: Addressing challenges posed by disruptions in global supply chains, such as during the COVID-19 pandemic.

Technological Advancements: Harnessing technological innovations to drive economic competitiveness and foster digital trade.

Sustainable Development: Balancing economic growth with sustainable practices to promote environmentally responsible trade.

Strengthening Economic Resilience

Economic Reforms: Analyzing the importance of economic reforms to enhance competitiveness and attract foreign direct investment.

Investment in Human Capital: Investing in education, skills development, and research to foster a skilled workforce and drive innovation.

SMEs and Inclusive Growth: Supporting small and medium-sized enterprises (SMEs) to foster inclusive economic growth and prosperity.

In "The New Power" era of 2024, Mexico's trade and economic partnerships are critical for the nation's economic prosperity and global standing. Embracing regional integration and diversification of trade partnerships will allow Mexico to harness opportunities in a rapidly changing global economy. Addressing challenges in supply chain disruptions and promoting sustainable practices will enhance economic resilience and competitiveness. By strengthening economic ties with emerging markets and investing in human capital, Mexico can position itself as a dynamic and influential player in the global economy. In "The New Power" era, Mexico has the opportunity to shape its economic destiny, leveraging trade and partnerships to drive sustainable growth and prosperity for its people.

IMPACT OF TRADE AGREEMENTS ON MEXICO'S ECONOMY

In "The New Power" era of 2024, trade agreements have played a pivotal role in shaping Mexico's economic landscape. As a nation deeply integrated into the global economy, Mexico's trade agreements have had a profound impact on its economic growth, industrial development, and international competitiveness. This chapter explores the significance of trade agreements for Mexico's economy, analyzing the benefits and challenges they bring to various sectors and the nation's overall economic well-being.

The United States-Mexico-Canada Agreement (USMCA)

Modernization of NAFTA: Understanding how the USMCA replaced the North American Free Trade Agreement (NAFTA) and the changes it brought.

Impact on Trade Flows: Analyzing the effects of the USMCA on trade volumes, tariffs, and market access for Mexican products.

Rules of Origin: Exploring the rules of origin and their implications for the automotive and manufacturing sectors.

Regional Trade Agreements

The Pacific Alliance: Assessing the benefits of Mexico's participation in the Pacific Alliance and the opportunities it creates for increased regional integration.

CPTPP: Understanding Mexico's involvement in the Comprehensive and Progressive Agreement for Trans-Pacific Partnership (CPTPP) and its potential impact on trade diversification.

Economic Sector Impacts

Agriculture: Analyzing the effects of trade agreements on Mexico's agricultural sector, including challenges faced by small-scale farmers.

Manufacturing and Automotive Industries: Exploring the impact of trade agreements on Mexico's manufacturing and automotive sectors, as well as the growth of supply chains.

Services and Digital Trade: Assessing how trade agreements facilitate services trade and digital commerce, contributing to Mexico's service-oriented economy.

Foreign Direct Investment (FDI)

Investment Inflows: Analyzing the impact of trade agreements on attracting foreign direct investment to Mexico.

Opportunities and Challenges: Understanding how trade agreements can create opportunities for domestic businesses while also presenting challenges for local industries.

Economic Growth and Competitiveness

GDP Growth: Examining the correlation between trade agreements and Mexico's overall economic growth.

Enhanced Competitiveness: Assessing how trade agreements have contributed to Mexico's improved competitiveness in the global market.

Socioeconomic Implications

Employment: Analyzing the effects of trade agreements on employment, job creation, and labor markets.

Income Inequality: Addressing the impact of trade agreements on income distribution and inequality.

In "The New Power" era of 2024, trade agreements continue to shape Mexico's economic fortunes and global integration. The USMCA and other regional trade agreements have opened new opportunities for trade, investment, and economic growth. While these agreements have brought numerous benefits, they also present challenges, particularly in certain economic sectors and socio-economic dimensions. By strategically leveraging trade agreements, Mexico can further enhance its economic competitiveness and prosperity. In "The New Power" era, Mexico has the chance to navigate the complexities of the global economy, harnessing the benefits of trade agreements to drive inclusive and sustainable growth for the betterment of its people and the nation as a whole.

STRENGTHENING BILATERAL AND MULTILATERAL RELATIONSHIPS

In "The New Power" era of 2024, strengthening bilateral and multilateral relationships is crucial for Mexico's role in the global arena. As the world becomes more interconnected, robust diplomatic ties with other nations and active participation in international organizations are essential for advancing Mexico's interests and addressing global challenges. This chapter explores Mexico's approach to enhancing its bilateral and multilateral relationships, focusing on the opportunities and benefits such collaborations can bring.

Bilateral Diplomacy

United States: Analyzing the significance of Mexico's relationship with the United States and the potential areas of collaboration.

Canada: Understanding the importance of Mexico's bilateral ties with Canada and opportunities for economic partnerships.

Latin American Partners: Exploring Mexico's relations with other Latin American countries and the potential for regional cooperation.

European Union: Assessing Mexico's engagement with the European Union and the opportunities for trade and investment.

Multilateral Diplomacy

United Nations (UN): Mexico's engagement with the UN and its role in global initiatives for peace, development, and human rights.

World Trade Organization (WTO): Analyzing Mexico's participation in the WTO and its efforts to advance free trade and resolve trade disputes.

G20 and Other Forums: Understanding Mexico's role in international forums such as the G20 and its contribution to global economic governance.

Promoting International Cooperation

Climate Change and Sustainable Development: Mexico's efforts to collaborate with other nations in addressing climate change and promoting sustainable development goals.

Security and Transnational Crime: Exploring Mexico's cooperation with other countries in combating transnational crime and ensuring regional security.

Humanitarian Assistance: Analyzing Mexico's contributions to humanitarian efforts and disaster relief in collaboration with other nations.

Economic Diplomacy

Investment Promotion: Strategies for attracting foreign investment and promoting Mexico as an attractive investment destination.

Market Access: Negotiating trade agreements and removing barriers to facilitate market access for Mexican products and services.

Soft Power and Cultural Diplomacy

Promoting Mexican Culture: Utilizing cultural diplomacy to enhance Mexico's soft power and build bridges with other nations.

Educational and Scientific Exchanges: Promoting educational and scientific exchanges to foster international cooperation and knowledge sharing.

In "The New Power" era of 2024, strengthening bilateral and multilateral relationships is essential for Mexico's prosperity and influence in the global community. By fostering robust diplomatic ties with key partners, actively engaging in multilateral forums, and collaborating on common challenges, Mexico can advance its economic, political, and social interests. Promoting international cooperation, economic diplomacy, and cultural exchange will enhance Mexico's soft power and solidify its position as an active and responsible global player. In "The New Power" era, Mexico has the opportunity to build strong alliances and partnerships, working towards a more interconnected and harmonious world.

THE NEW POWER IN ACTION GRASSROOTS MOVEMENTS AND CIVIL SOCIETY INITIATIVES

In "The New Power" era of 2024, grassroots movements and civil society initiatives have emerged as powerful agents of change in Mexico's political landscape. These movements, driven by passionate citizens and non-governmental organizations, advocate for various social, environmental, and political causes. This chapter delves into the significance of grassroots movements and civil society initiatives, their impact on shaping public policies, and their role in fostering an inclusive and participatory democracy.

The Rise of Grassroots Movements

Social Movements: Analyzing the emergence of social movements advocating for human rights, gender equality, indigenous rights, and social justice.

Environmental Activism: Understanding the role of environmental movements in addressing climate change, conservation, and sustainability.

Student Activism: Exploring the influence of student movements on education reform, youth empowerment, and political participation.

Civil Society Initiatives

NGO Sector: Assessing the contributions of non-governmental organizations (NGOs) in promoting transparency, accountability, and human rights.

Community-Based Organizations: Understanding the impact of community-based initiatives in addressing local challenges and promoting development.

Social Entrepreneurship: Exploring the role of social entrepreneurs in driving innovative solutions to societal issues.

Civil Society and Policy Advocacy

Influencing Public Policy: Analyzing how grassroots movements and civil society organizations advocate for policy changes and social reforms.

Participatory Democracy: Understanding the role of civil society in promoting citizen engagement and participatory decision-making.

Government-Civil Society Collaboration: Assessing the opportunities and challenges in collaboration between civil society and government institutions.

Digital Activism and Online Mobilization

Social Media Impact: Analyzing the influence of social media platforms in mobilizing and amplifying grassroots movements' messages.

Online Advocacy Campaigns: Exploring how digital activism drives awareness and mobilizes support for various causes.

Challenges and Opportunities

Funding and Sustainability: Addressing the challenges of funding and sustaining grassroots movements and civil society initiatives.

Government Response: Analyzing the relationship between civil society and the government and its implications for activism.

Inclusivity and Diversity: Emphasizing the importance of inclusivity and diversity in grassroots movements to ensure representation and broad support.

In "The New Power" era of 2024, grassroots movements and civil society initiatives have become transformative forces in Mexico's political and social landscape. As the voice of the people, they bring critical issues to the forefront, advocate for change, and contribute to shaping public policies. Digital activism and online mobilization have expanded their reach, amplified their messages and galvanized public support. However, challenges persist in sustaining these movements and ensuring their inclusivity and effectiveness. In "The New Power" era, empowering and supporting grassroots movements and civil society initiatives is crucial for promoting an inclusive and participatory democracy, fostering social progress, and advancing the aspirations of the people. Through collaboration between citizens, civil society, and government, Mexico can create a society where the collective voice of its people drives positive change and a better future for all.

THE ROLE OF CIVIL SOCIETY IN MEXICAN POLITICS

In "The New Power" era of 2024, civil society has emerged as a pivotal player in shaping Mexican politics and society. As an independent and diverse sector, civil society organizations (CSOs) and grassroots movements play a crucial role in advocating for the interests of citizens, promoting transparency, and holding the government accountable. This chapter explores the multifaceted role of civil society in Mexican politics, its contributions to democracy, and the challenges it faces in the pursuit of a more inclusive and participatory political landscape.

Defining Civil Society in Mexico

Non-Governmental Organizations (NGOs): Understanding the diverse range of NGOs and their areas of focus, from human rights to environmental conservation.

Social Movements and Grassroots Initiatives: Analyzing the rise of social movements and grassroots initiatives advocating for various causes and policy changes.

Media and Advocacy Groups: Exploring the role of media organizations and advocacy groups in promoting public awareness and policy advocacy.

Advancing Democracy and Political Participation

Citizen Engagement: The significance of civil society in fostering citizen engagement and promoting active political participation.

Advocating for Electoral Reforms: Analyzing civil society's efforts in advocating for electoral reforms to strengthen the democratic process.

Election Monitoring and Transparency: The role of civil society in election monitoring to ensure free and fair elections and maintain transparency.

Promoting Human Rights and Social Justice

Human Rights Advocacy: The impact of civil society organizations in advocating for human rights protection and holding perpetrators accountable.

Gender Equality and LGBTQ+ Rights: Analyzing civil society's role in promoting gender equality and LGBTQ+ rights in Mexican society.

Indigenous Rights and Cultural Preservation: Understanding civil society's efforts in preserving the rights and cultural heritage of indigenous communities.

Holding Government Accountable

Anti-Corruption Efforts: Exploring civil society's contributions to combatting corruption and promoting transparency in government.

Citizen Monitoring and Oversight: The role of civil society in monitoring government actions and expenditures.

Policy Advocacy and Public Policy Formation: Analyzing how civil society influences policy formation through advocacy and public mobilization.

Collaborations and Challenges

Government-Civil Society Relations: Assessing the dynamics of collaboration and tension between civil society and government institutions.

Funding and Sustainability: Addressing the challenges of funding and sustainability faced by civil society organizations.

Inclusivity and Representation: Emphasizing the importance of ensuring diverse representation within civil society to effectively address societal issues.

In "The New Power" era of 2024, civil society plays a vital role in Mexico's political landscape, advocating for human rights, social justice, and government accountability. As a crucial voice of the people, civil society organizations and grassroots movements drive positive change and promote an inclusive democracy. Challenges of funding, sustainability, and inclusivity require collective efforts to overcome. By fostering collaborative relationships with the government and promoting active citizen engagement, civil society can continue to drive progress and contribute to a more responsive and participatory political system. In "The New Power" era, Mexico has the opportunity to strengthen civil society's role and amplify the collective voice of its people for a more equitable and empowered society.

CASE STUDIES OF SUCCESSFUL GRASSROOTS MOVEMENTS

In "The New Power" era of 2024, grassroots movements have become powerful catalysts for change in Mexico's political landscape. These movements, driven by passionate citizens and civil society organizations, have successfully advocated for various causes, leading to transformative policy changes and societal progress. This chapter examines case studies of successful grassroots movements in Mexico, highlighting their impact, strategies, and lessons learned.

#NiUnaMenos - Combating Gender-Based Violence

Context and Objectives: Analyzing the origins and objectives of the #NiUnaMenos movement in addressing gender-based violence and femicide.

Public Mobilization: Understanding the movement's strategies for mobilizing public support and raising awareness of gender-related issues.

Policy Impact: Assessing the movement's influence on policy changes, legal reforms, and government commitment to combating gender-based violence.

#FridaysForFuture - Environmental Activism

Climate Activism in Mexico: Examining how the #FridaysForFuture movement mobilized youth and citizens to demand action on climate change.

Grassroots Campaigns: Analyzing the movement's grassroots campaigns and digital advocacy for climate action and environmental protection.

Advocacy for Policy Reforms: Understanding the movement's role in influencing Mexico's climate policies and promoting sustainability.

#YoSoy132 - Youth Empowerment and Political Participation

Youth Mobilization: Analyzing how the #YoSoy132 movement mobilized young citizens to engage in the political process and demand transparency.

Social Media and Citizen Journalism: Understanding the role of social media and citizen journalism in amplifying the movement's message.

Impact on Electoral Politics: Assessing the movement's impact on the 2012 presidential election and subsequent political discourse.

Zapatista Movement - Indigenous Rights and Autonomy

Indigenous Activism: Examining the Zapatista movement's struggle for indigenous rights and autonomy in Chiapas.

Mobilization and Community Building: Understanding the movement's community-based approach to empowerment and social change.

International Solidarity: Analyzing the Zapatistas' engagement with global civil society and their influence on indigenous rights movements worldwide.

#VivasNosQueremos - Women's Rights and Safety

Addressing Gender-Based Violence: Analyzing the #VivasNosQueremos movement's efforts to address femicide and violence against women.

Public Demonstrations: Understanding the movement's use of public demonstrations and art activism to demand justice and safety for women.

Impact on Policy and Awareness: Assessing the movement's impact on public awareness and policy changes related to gender-based violence.

In "The New Power" era of 2024, these case studies of successful grassroots movements in Mexico demonstrate the transformative power of civil society in shaping the nation's political and social landscape. These movements have not only brought critical issues to the forefront but also influenced policy changes, promoted inclusivity, and empowered citizens to be active agents of change. Through mobilization, digital advocacy, and community engagement, grassroots movements have driven progress in environmental protection, gender equality, indigenous rights, and political participation. By studying these successful case studies, Mexico can draw valuable lessons on the effectiveness of grassroots activism, the power of social mobilization, and the importance of fostering an inclusive and participatory democracy. In "The New Power" era, Mexico has the opportunity to support and amplify the voices of civil society to build a more equitable and empowered society for all its citizens.

MEDIA AND POLITICAL DISCOURSE

In "The New Power" era of 2024, the media plays a pivotal role in shaping Mexico's political landscape and influencing public opinion. As a key platform for disseminating information, media outlets hold significant power in framing political discourse, shaping public perceptions, and holding political actors accountable. This chapter explores the interplay between media and politics in Mexico, examining the role of traditional and digital media, the challenges of media independence, and the impact of media on political participation.

Media Landscape in Mexico

Traditional Media Outlets: Analyzing the dominance and influence of traditional media such as television, radio, and newspapers.

Digital Media and Social Networks: Understanding the rise of digital media platforms and social networks as powerful tools for political communication.

Media Ownership and Independence: Assessing the impact of media ownership on editorial independence and media freedom.

Framing Political Discourse

Media Agenda Setting: Understanding how the media influence's public opinion by setting the agenda on political issues.

Political Reporting and Bias: Analyzing the role of media bias in shaping the narrative around political events and personalities.

Influence of Opinion Leaders and Pundits: Examining the impact of opinion leaders and political pundits on public perceptions.

Role in Elections and Political Campaigns

Media Coverage of Elections: Understanding how the media covers electoral campaigns and its impact on voter behavior.

Political Advertising: Analyzing the role of political advertising in shaping public perceptions of candidates and parties.

Media Regulations and Fairness: Assessing the effectiveness of media regulations in ensuring fair and balanced coverage during elections.

Challenges and Opportunities

Fake News and Misinformation: Addressing the challenge of fake news and misinformation in the digital age.

Media Censorship and Freedom of Expression: Analyzing the impact of media censorship on political discourse and freedom of expression.

Media Literacy and Critical Thinking: Promoting media literacy and critical thinking to empower citizens in navigating media information.

Media and Political Participation

Media as a Tool for Citizen Engagement: Exploring how media can facilitate citizen engagement and political participation.

Role of Citizen Journalism: Understanding the role of citizen journalism in democratizing information dissemination.

Media and Social Movements: Analyzing how media coverage influences the dynamics of social movements and political advocacy.

In "The New Power" era of 2024, media and political discourse are intertwined, with the media serving as a crucial mediator between politics and citizens. By shaping public opinion, setting the political agenda, and providing information, the media influences political decisions and public engagement. However, challenges such as media bias, misinformation, and censorship must be addressed to ensure a healthy democratic discourse. Media literacy and critical thinking are essential for citizens to navigate the media landscape effectively and engage in informed political participation. As Mexico embraces "The New Power" era, promoting media freedom, independence, and responsible journalism will foster an informed and engaged citizenry, driving a more transparent and inclusive political system. By harnessing the potential of media as a tool for democracy, Mexico can strengthen its democratic institutions and empower its people to actively participate in shaping the nation's future.

MEDIA LANDSCAPE AND ITS INFLUENCE ON POLITICS

In "The New Power" era of 2024, the media landscape in Mexico is more diverse and influential than ever before. Media outlets, both traditional and digital, wield considerable power in shaping political narratives, influencing public opinion, and setting the agenda for political discourse. This chapter examines the evolving media landscape in Mexico and its profound influence on politics, analyzing the role of media ownership, media bias, digital platforms, and the impact of media on political decision-making.

Traditional Media and Its Reach

Television: Understanding the dominance of television as the primary source of news and political information for the Mexican population.

Radio and Print Media: Analyzing the influence of radio and newspapers in shaping regional and local political narratives.

Ownership and Editorial Independence: Assessing the influence of media ownership on editorial independence and the potential for media bias.

Digital Media and the Rise of Social Networks

Digital Platforms: Exploring the rise of digital media platforms and their impact on the dissemination of news and information.

Social Media and Political Engagement: Analyzing how social media platforms have transformed political communication and citizen engagement.

Influence of Social Media Influencers: Understanding the role of social media influencers in shaping public perceptions and political discourse.

Media Bias and Framing

Media Bias in Reporting: Analyzing the presence of media bias and its impact on political reporting.

Framing of Political Events: Understanding how media framing influences public perceptions of political events and issues.

Political Spin and Messaging: Assessing the role of political spin in shaping media coverage and public opinion.

Media and Political Campaigns

Political Advertising: Analyzing the use of media in political advertising during electoral campaigns.

Media Coverage of Political Candidates: Understanding how media coverage influences voter perceptions of political candidates.

Media Debates and Candidate Performances: Examining the impact of media debates on voter decision-making.

Media Influence on Political Decision-Making

Agenda Setting: Understanding how the media sets the political agenda and shapes public priorities.

Policy Impact: Analyzing the media's influence on political decision-making and policy formation.

Media Accountability and Holding Politicians Responsible: Assessing the media's role in holding politicians accountable for their actions and decisions.

In "The New Power" era of 2024, the media landscape in Mexico is a critical factor in shaping politics and public opinion. From traditional media outlets like television and print to the rise of digital platforms and social media, media plays a central role in political discourse and decision-making. Media bias, framing, and political advertising can significantly influence public perceptions and voter behavior. As Mexico navigates this dynamic media environment, promoting media freedom, independence, and responsible journalism is crucial for fostering an informed and engaged citizenry. By embracing the potential of media as a tool for transparency, accountability, and citizen empowerment, Mexico can strengthen its democratic institutions and ensure that the media serves as a powerful force for positive change in the nation's political landscape.

PROMOTING RESPONSIBLE JOURNALISM AND INFORMATION INTEGRITY

In "The New Power" era of 2024, responsible journalism and information integrity are paramount in shaping Mexico's political landscape and fostering an informed citizenry. The media, as a powerful conduit of information, has a significant role in shaping public opinion and political discourse. This chapter delves into the importance of promoting responsible journalism, combating misinformation, and upholding information integrity for the betterment of Mexico's democratic society.

The Role of Journalism in Democracy

Fourth Estate: Understanding the crucial role of journalism as the fourth estate, holding power to account and informing the public.

Ethical Principles: Analyzing the ethical principles and standards that journalists must adhere to, such as accuracy, fairness, and impartiality.

Media as a Public Good: Recognizing the media's role as a public good, serving the public interest and promoting transparency.

Combating Misinformation and Fake News

The Challenge of Misinformation: Addressing the growing problem of misinformation and its impact on public opinion.

Fact-Checking and Verification: Understanding the importance of fact-checking and verification in combating fake news.

Media Literacy Education: Promoting media literacy education to empower citizens in discerning reliable information from misinformation.

Transparency and Information Integrity

Source Transparency: Advocating for transparency in media reporting, including clear attribution and sourcing.

Editorial Independence: Ensuring editorial independence to safeguard media organizations from undue influence.

Media Ownership Disclosure: Analyzing the importance of disclosing media ownership to promote transparency.

Journalistic Freedom and Safety

Freedom of Press: Upholding and defending the freedom of the press as a pillar of a democratic society.

Protection of Journalists: Addressing the safety and protection of journalists in their pursuit of truth.

Journalist Ethics and Responsibility: Emphasizing the role of journalists in responsibly reporting and avoiding sensationalism.

Collaboration and Industry Initiatives

Collaboration against Misinformation: Promoting collaboration between media organizations and technology platforms to combat misinformation.

Media Integrity Initiatives: Understanding industry-led initiatives to promote media integrity and responsible reporting.

Engaging the Public: Encouraging media organizations to engage with the public and be responsive to audience feedback.

In "The New Power" era of 2024, promoting responsible journalism and information integrity is essential for nurturing a healthy and informed democracy in Mexico. By upholding ethical principles, combating misinformation, and ensuring transparency, the media can play a crucial role in informing citizens and holding those in power accountable. Media literacy education is vital for empowering the public to be critical consumers of information. Through collaboration, industry initiatives, and public engagement, media organizations can strengthen their credibility and foster public trust. As Mexico navigates a dynamic media landscape, embracing responsible journalism will contribute to a more transparent, participatory, and resilient democracy. In "The New Power" era, Mexico has the opportunity to champion responsible journalism, safeguarding the public's right to accurate and reliable information for the betterment of its democratic society.

CONCLUSION

MEXICO'S PATH FORWARD: TOWARDS A NEW POWER IN 2024 AND BEYOND

In "The New Power" era of 2024, Mexico stands at a critical juncture in its political journey. This book has explored various facets of Mexico's politics, from its historical evolution to the challenges and opportunities it faces today. As the nation charts its path forward, this concluding chapter reflects on the key themes discussed and outlines Mexico's potential for a new era of political empowerment and progress.

Political Evolution and Democratization

Mexico's political landscape has undergone significant transformations, transitioning from an authoritarian regime to a vibrant democracy. The journey towards democratization has been marked by struggles for human rights, civil liberties, and political participation. While notable progress has been made, challenges of corruption, crime, and social inequality persist.

The Role of Civil Society and Grassroots Movements

In "The New Power" era, civil society and grassroots movements have emerged as powerful agents of change. From advocating for human rights and social justice to promoting environmental protection, these movements amplify the voice of the people and hold power to account. Embracing their influence is vital for building a more inclusive and responsive political system.

Media Landscape and Public Discourse

The media plays a central role in shaping political narratives and influencing public opinion. Ensuring responsible journalism, combating misinformation, and promoting media freedom are essential for fostering an informed and engaged citizenry. As Mexico navigates the digital age, leveraging digital media for transparency and public engagement can strengthen its democratic foundation.

Institutional Reforms and Anti-Corruption Efforts

Effective governance relies on robust institutions and anti-corruption measures. Continued efforts to reform institutions, enhance transparency, and combat corruption are essential for building public trust and ensuring the equitable distribution of resources.

Empowering Youth and Education

Empowering the youth is crucial for securing Mexico's future. Investing in education, skills development, and youth participation in politics can foster a more vibrant and dynamic society. Empowered youth bring fresh perspectives, innovative ideas, and drive positive change.

Foreign Policy and Global Engagement

Mexico's foreign policy plays a significant role in shaping its global standing and addressing transnational challenges. Strengthening international cooperation, promoting trade and economic partnerships, and advocating for human rights on the global stage can enhance Mexico's influence and contribution to global affairs.

As "The New Power" era unfolds in 2024 and beyond, Mexico has the opportunity to harness its rich history, diverse culture, and the resilience of its people to overcome challenges and drive progress. Nurturing a participatory democracy, empowering civil society, and ensuring responsible governance are critical for achieving a more prosperous and just society. By embracing transparency, combating corruption, and promoting information integrity, Mexico can fortify the foundations of its democracy and build public trust.

In the pursuit of a more inclusive future, Mexico must prioritize education, youth empowerment, and sustainable development. Embracing technology and digital platforms can amplify the voices of its citizens, foster social change, and connect with the global community.

The path forward for Mexico lies in collaborative efforts between government, civil society, and citizens to address complex issues and build a collective vision for the nation's progress. In "The New Power" era, Mexico's journey is not predetermined, and the actions taken today will shape the nation's future. As the nation strides towards a brighter tomorrow, it must remember that the power lies within its people, united in purpose and determined to create a more prosperous and equitable Mexico.

EPILOGUE

REFLECTIONS ON "THE NEW POWER 2024" AND BUILDING A BETTER MEXICO

In this concluding chapter, we reflect on the journey through "The New Power" era of 2024 in Mexico's politics. We examine the milestones achieved, the challenges faced, and the collective vision for a better Mexico. As the nation looks ahead, the epilogue emphasizes the importance of unity, inclusivity, and active citizen engagement in building a prosperous and equitable future.

Celebrating Achievements and Progress

"The New Power" era has witnessed remarkable achievements in Mexico's political landscape. From the rise of civil society movements to policy reforms and advancements in technology, the nation has embraced new dynamics of governance and public engagement. Celebrating these accomplishments serves as a reminder of the potential for positive change when individuals and communities unite for a common cause.

Acknowledging Challenges and Unfinished Business

Despite the progress, Mexico still grapples with critical challenges. Corruption, crime, social inequality, and environmental degradation require sustained efforts and collaborative solutions. Acknowledging the hurdles ahead is essential for developing comprehensive strategies that address the root causes of these issues.

The Power of Collaboration and Inclusivity

"The New Power" era has demonstrated the transformative power of collaboration and inclusivity. In embracing diversity and engaging citizens from all walks of life, Mexico can harness collective wisdom and strength to create innovative solutions to its most pressing challenges.

Nurturing Democratic Values

A robust democracy is built on democratic values such as transparency, accountability, and respect for human rights. Fostering a culture that upholds these values is vital for a thriving democratic society where citizens are actively engaged in shaping their future.

Youth as Agents of Change

The youth of Mexico hold immense potential as agents of change. Empowering young citizens through quality education, skills development, and meaningful political participation is pivotal for a dynamic and progressive nation.

Embracing Technology for Progress

Technological advancements have the capacity to reshape governance, public discourse, and civic engagement. Embracing technology responsibly and leveraging it for transparent governance and citizen empowerment can unlock new possibilities for Mexico's progress.

A Vision for the Future

As Mexico looks to the future, a collective vision must be crafted, transcending political divisions and vested interests. This vision should be rooted in a commitment to sustainable development, social justice, and inclusive prosperity for all.

Active Citizenship and Civic Responsibility

Building a better Mexico requires active citizenship and civic responsibility. Engaging in constructive dialogue, participating in democratic processes, and holding leaders accountable are the hallmarks of an empowered citizenry.

Embracing "The New Power" Beyond 2024

"The New Power" era of 2024 is not a finite period but a continuous journey of progress and transformation. Embracing the principles of "The New Power" beyond 2024 ensures that the vision for a better Mexico endures for generations to come.

In this epilogue, we reflect on the impact of "The New Power" era in Mexico's politics and society. We celebrate the achievements, acknowledge the challenges, and underscore the importance of unity, inclusivity, and active citizenship in building a prosperous and equitable nation. As Mexico moves forward, it must remain committed to the democratic values that empower its people and foster a more resilient and vibrant society. The journey towards a better Mexico requires collective effort, shared vision, and an unwavering commitment to the principles of "The New Power." In the spirit of progress, let us embrace the future with hope, determination, and a shared belief in the limitless potential of Mexico's people and its democratic spirit. Together, we can build a better Mexico - a nation that stands as a beacon of democracy, justice, and prosperity for all.

ABOUT THE AUTHOR

"The New Power 2024: Politics in Mexico" is a compelling exploration of Mexico's political landscape and its journey towards a brighter future. As readers delve into the complexities of Mexico's politics and society, it is essential to understand the background and expertise of the author who penned this insightful book. Over the years, King Rojo has accumulated extensive experience in the field of political analysis and international relations. Their expertise has been honed through research, consulting, and advisory roles with renowned think tanks, academic institutions, and government bodies. Through these experiences, they have cultivated a unique perspective on Mexico's political evolution and its place in the global arena.

Meet the Author

King Rojo